With Love...

Janis Amatuzio MD

# FOREVER OURS

# FOREVER OURS

A forensic pathologist's perspective
on immortality and living

A COLLECTION OF REAL-LIFE STORIES

## Janis Amatuzio, M.D.

Minneapolis, Minnesota

Publisher: Midwest Forensic Pathology, P.A., 3960 Coon Rapids Blvd., LL21, Coon Rapids, Minnesota 55433, 763-236-9050, foreverours.com

Editor: Sherri Weiss
Cover design: Amy Kirkpatrick
Cover illustration: Illustration Works, Inc., Darren Hopes/Amy Kirkpatrick
Author photograph: Mike Kelcher
Book design: Dorie McClelland, Spring Type & Design
Printed in U.S.A.

Publisher's Cataloging-in-Publication
*(Provided by Quality Books, Inc.)*

Amatuzio, Janis.
     Forever ours : a forensic pathologist's perspective on immortality and living-- a collection of real-life stories / Janis Amatuzio. -- 1st ed.
     p.cm.

     1. Grief--Case studies. 2. Bereavement--Psychological aspects--Case studies. 3. Spirituality. 4. Family.   I. Title.

BF575.G7.A43 2001              155.937
                               QB133-166

ISBN: 0-9716287-0-X


05  04  03      5  4  3

For my mother and father, Verda and Don,
whose love has encouraged me to dream
and to live life to its fullest

For all those who love
and grieve

And for all who have taught me
what really heals.

# Contents

# *Foreword*

## A LETTER FROM JOHN R. HASTINGS, M.D.

March 28, 2001

Dear Dr. Amatuzio,

Thank you for bringing your stories to me so that I could read them. As you know, I am currently wrestling with my own perception of mortality. I found that your writings helped me and gave me a sense of comfort.

The stories you have collected and so eloquently written represent, I believe, an effort to search for core human beliefs.

My own search is for a set of realities which will help me deal with my own critical illness. My basic convictions include life after death and forgiveness. While it's useful to read about these concepts in various scriptures and other sources of "knowledge," I've found that "first hand accounts" illuminate and lend credence to my personal set of ideas.

. . . However, personally, the two pieces that made the greatest impression on me were "The Visit" and "The Tapestry of Life."

In "The Visit," I was struck by an "out of body experience" which bridged the world of things we can touch, feel, and see with the world of the intangible.

"The Tapestry of Life" is an elegant closing chapter for your book. It has brought me comfort at a time of personal trial and testing. Your words have prompted me to expedite closure with members of my personal family as my medical condition progresses.

Additionally, I am looking at encounters which lend sincerity to my belief that there is an afterlife that has the ability to interact with what I would describe as "worldly time."

Finally, I thank you for allowing me the privilege to read your book before its publication and for the amazing and helpful insights it offers.

Sincerely,

John R. Hastings, M.D.


POSTSCRIPT: Dr. Hastings, a fellow pathologist, died on June 19, 2001, at age 56, of thyroid cancer. I thank him for the courage and wisdom he brought into my life, and for permission to use his letter.

# Acknowledgments

The stories in this book are real. In some stories, the actual names and circumstances have been used with permission. In others, names and circumstances have been changed to protect privacy.

I am incredibly grateful to all who shared their stories and allowed them to be told. These stories have been like treasures, collected, one by one over the years, written on scraps of paper and envelope backs or stuffed in a file folder. It has taken the love, attention, and encouragement of many to cause this book to be written, crafted, and published. A few of these people include:

Lori Allert, RN, Major, U.S. Army Reserve, a forensic nurse; and my dear friend and colleague who gathered the handwritten paper scraps and lovingly typed them into the very first draft. She poured over every story, encouraged me, pushed aside my doubts and listened. She epitomizes the words of Kahlil Gibran, "You save your best for your friend."

Kathleen McMonigal, M.D., Director of Diagnostic Services for Space Medicine, National Aeronautics and Space Administration, Johnson Space Center, Houston, Texas, pathologist, and my dear friend and confidante, who began gently listening to these stories so many years ago, in Sante Fe, New Mexico, storing them in her heart, and encouraging me to write the "next grandest version." Her wisdom, love, and wit grace my life like a beautiful gemstone.

Gregg Mekler, my powerful friend and beloved life advisor.

Kay Cooper, my dear friend and office manager who has artfully managed the details of my life and work so that I could devote the time to writing. Dr. Huston, Dr. Bandt, and Mel, and my wonderful office staff, Marilyn, Karen, Sue, and Bob, who cheerfully facilitated my every request.

Patricia Amatuzio and Chris Bohler, my marvelous sister and brother-in-law, who focused my imagination with their laughter, love, and skill.

Dorie McClelland, my book designer, whose generous spirit, warmth, and creative genius framed these words with her beautiful designs.

Sherri Weiss, my editor, whose skills honed the stories and set them on fire.

Tom Baumgart, my most wonderful husband, splendid companion, and friend—your love is my greatest treasure.

Many thanks also to my family, including Barry, Paula, and Samantha, and friends (too numerous to list) whose names are written in my heart.

# PART I

# IN THE BEGINNING

❦

I used to say:
we teach that which
we most need to learn.

Now I say:
we teach that which
we most need to remember.

*Janis Amatuzio*

# SEEDS OF HOPE

**M**y mother, my great encourager and supporter, listened patiently as I read her the last chapter of this book and did what every daughter prays for in such a moment. She cried and then looked at me with such an expression of admiration and pride. As my mother gave me this gift, she asked a question that would give me one more. She said, "Janis, it's just beautiful, but tell me something . . . for whom did you write this book, and more importantly, why?"

I felt the familiar tug in my heart, the one that lets me know there is more to learn and more to understand. I had to dig deeply for the answers, some of which surprised me. Let me explain.

Simply put, I am a physician. Specifically, a forensic pathologist; one who speaks for the dead. As a county coroner or medical examiner, I have spent years documenting and describing death scenes, examining bodies, and performing autopsies. I have carefully counted stab wounds, photographed gunshot wounds, and traced the pathways of injuries through the body.

The forensic pathologist must answer the question, "What happened?", and explain the answer clearly and scientifically to the courts, to law enforcement, to physicians, and most of all to the family of the deceased person.

I grew up watching my physician father, an internist, take time to talk with and kindly listen to his patients. Perhaps that's why I began talking with and listening to the families of deceased persons who received my care. I made it a practice to call the family members and explain the autopsy results on noncriminal cases, send a letter, and, when needed, meet in person.

These talks have not always been easy for me. After explaining the autopsy results, toxicology results, and conclusions that forensic pathology can provide, I inevitably come face to face with the family's raw grief, their tears and torn hearts, and the question that I can never answer— "why?"

But the exact thing that brought me the greatest unease also brought me the greatest gift. These families, the loved ones left behind, have occasionally shared their perspectives and thoughts and sometimes the dreams, visions, and synchronicities experienced in and around the death of their loved ones. These reflections have made me wonder.

When I was growing up and didn't understand a problem or an issue, I would often talk with my father and be told to study harder. Applying this wisdom, I began to study the issue of death and loss and mortality from every angle I could imagine. It's been written that if you look at something closely enough, you begin to see right through it. I have come to believe that the answers to life's most difficult questions are woven into its design, much like an optical illusion.

First, you have to be looking and when you look closely enough, something happens—a tiny shift in perspective occurs. Images once hidden become apparent, and you can't help but wonder what changed and why you didn't recognize them before.

I've come to realize that there is a mysterious dimension of forensic pathology that I almost missed entirely, and yet it also feels strangely familiar. Although I still document the "body of evidence," I have become fascinated with "the essence of what left." The problem, however, for a scientist and physician is that this field isn't precise. It can't be measured or photographed and it can't be proven beyond a reasonable degree of medical certainty. It has required me to take a leap—a huge leap professionally—from my mind to my heart. To do so is to remember that what is most meaningful often cannot be measured and that everything that counts cannot be counted.

Individually, these experiences and shared stories were interesting, but collectively they had the ring of a larger truth. Almost unexpectedly, and much like an optical illusion, as I gathered and wrote these stories, I realized that the answers I had been searching for had been there all along. They were woven into the fabric of my patients' lives and deaths and woven into my own. I just hadn't recognized it.

So, to answer my mother's first question, I realize now that I wrote this book for myself. You see, I believe that you teach that which you need most to learn. And I now know that we teach that which we need most to remember. That perhaps is the greatest revelation for me. The answers were there all along. I just had to remember them.

The answer to the second question, "why?", is still unfolding, but is beginning to be replaced with wonder and inklings of greater things to come. The search has led me on an unexpected journey, and I have encountered some treasures along the way. I have grown much more aware of the Divine Presence in the Universe than I ever imagined. I remember more often to see the magic unfolding in my life. I have begun to trust that I am never alone. I have come to believe that our loved ones are truly "Forever Ours."

It has been said that what you do for another you ultimately do for yourself. These gathered experiences and recounted stories have been a blessing in my life. It is my fondest hope that the telling will be a blessing in yours.

# THE FIRST HOUSE CALL

I grew up watching my father care for people, attempt to heal them, and comfort them. I grew up watching my mother lovingly care for Dad and for us.

My father is a doctor and my mother a nurse. They met for the first time over the bed of a sick child on station 42, the pediatrics ward, at the University of Minnesota Hospitals in Minneapolis. Dad tells me how he knew in an instant that this pretty little Irish woman would one day be his wife. Three years later, in the midst of his internal medicine internship and World War II, they married and he went off to war. They wrote to one another every day. My mother has kept those love letters close to her heart all these years, carefully wrapped and stored with other treasures in her cedar chest.

When Dad returned from his tour of duty at a navy hospital in the Pacific, they began raising their family. I am the oldest of three children. I knew very early in my life that I would be a doctor (or a cowboy—my mother first convinced me that I was a girl, and then, that if I became a doctor, I might be able to afford being a cowgirl!)

Dad practiced medicine in the days before managed health care—when house calls were not uncommon. He never seemed to mind.

When I was a little girl, my father would take us along on house calls. I loved to go, but Dad would have my brother and me wait in the car while he went in to care for the sick. I often wondered just exactly what Dad did when he visited his patients, many of whom were our neighbors.

Mother tells me that one windy day while we were waiting in the car, Dad came out of a house to find that I had taken a whole box of tissues and let them go, one by one, out the car window. All of the lawns down the block were strewn with white floral tissues. Dad spent the next halfhour picking them up. After that, I never played with the tissues again, and I began to make house calls, too.

These visits fascinated me; even then I was aware that Dad seemed to be able to fix things. I would see looks of concern and worry melt into smiles and thank-you's. These people seemed to just love my dad.

It was amazing. I knew even then that part of the magic

that surrounded my father was his great compassion and his ability to gently reassure his patients. I know now that Dad reassured us all.

I remember that my father's doctor bag was made of smooth tan-brown leather. It had many compartments and smelled of antiseptics and leather polish. His stethoscope and blood-pressure cuff were nestled among papers and syringes and vials. I would often carry his bag as far as the patient's front door.

One day I went with my father to visit Mr. Phillips, an elderly neighbor who lived with his wife across the street from us. Their white house was filled with dark furniture, embroidered chairs, and heavy drapery. The house smelled of old things and perfume. Mrs. Phillips must have been watching for us because the front door opened before we climbed to the top step. She thanked Dad for coming to their home and held onto his hand as she told him about her husband, who had been sick for a long time. Dad put down his doctor's bag, took off his coat, and placed it on a hallway chair. "Don't worry now Irene. Let me go and see him. Janis, you wait here for me," he said as he gestured to one of the living room chairs.

Mrs. Phillips took Dad and his bag down the short dark hallway just off the living room and opened up a partly closed bedroom door. She came out a few  minutes later. I remember that she looked calmer than before. "Would you like some milk or lemonade?" she asked me. "Yes," I nodded as we walked into the kitchen and I sat down at the table. I remember how different their kitchen looked from my mother's. There was so much "stuff" on the counters—little bags of this and that, cookies and crackers, jams and nuts, and books everywhere. Mr. Phillips was a teacher. She placed a glass of cold milk and a plate of cookies in front of me. "How is Mr. Phillips?" I asked. "He is very sick," she answered.

"I'm so glad that your father is here to help him." She picked up an armload of towels from the floor. "Will you be alright here for a few minutes? I have to run downstairs for a moment to change a load of wash." I nodded and Mrs. Phillips disappeared down a narrow set of stairs to the basement.

I remember that I looked around, then quietly got off the chair and stole through the living room and down the hall to Mr. Phillips' bedroom. I peeked through a crack in the door. Mr. Phillips was sitting up in bed, his shirt was off, and Dad was thoughtfully listening to his chest, telling him to take a deep breath. Then Dad sat down beside the bed as

Mr. Phillips put his shirt back on. I saw Dad nod his head as Mr. Phillips began to speak. Then to my surprise, I saw Mr. Phillips put his big gnarled hand up to his eyes and begin to cry. They were great big sobs—his shoulders shook and his head was bowed. Dad gently reached over and put his hand on Mr. Phillips' arm, then took his hand and held it in both of his. Nobody talked for awhile. Mr. Phillips looked very old and boney just then, his skin thin and wrinkled. He seemed to all but disappear beneath the bedsheets. He and Dad sat there for a long time it seemed, and Mr. Phillips slowly stopped crying and reached over to Dad and hugged him. As Dad stood up I saw that he had tears in his eyes, too!

That was the first time I had seen my father cry. Then, I heard a noise and quickly ran back to the kitchen, gulped down the glass of milk, and hid a cookie in my pocket—just in time, as Mrs. Phillips was carrying a laundry basket of clothes up from the basement.

Dad spoke to her as we put on our coats to leave. She hugged him, too. They spoke in hushed tones as she wiped her eyes with her apron.

We left and, as we walked down the sidewalk, I remember taking Dad's hand and asking, "What is wrong with Mr. Phillips? He seems very sick and Mrs. Phillips is very worried about him. Will he get better?" Dad paused. "I don't think so Jombasba. This is a disease called Parkinson's, and he has had it for a very long time." (Jombasba was Dad's special name for me . . . derived from our Italian ancestry and from his imagination I think.) "But Dad, will he die?" Dad stopped right there in the middle of the sidewalk, looked a little sad, and said, "Yes, Mr. Phillips will eventually die. We all die someday Janis." My 9-year-old eyes filled with tears. "But Daddy, that's not right! Mrs. Phillips loves him so! Oh, this is just terrible!" I remember feeling overwhelmed and sat right down on the sidewalk and began to cry. My father seemed a bit flustered at my reaction, or perhaps he may have been a bit worried at what my mother would say. I felt as though I had just discovered a terrible secret.

Dad put his arms around me and said, "Janis what do you think happens when we die?" "I don't know," I sniveled, looking up at him, feeling miserable, and hoping once again that he could make things better. "Jombasba, we go to heaven—we go to be with God." "Where is heaven, Daddy?" My father took a deep breath, paused, and said, "Well you have to close your eyes and imagine the happiest, grandest, best place that you can, where all the special people and animals in your life are gathered, where the sky is velvet blue, the grass glistens, and the flowers smile, and you feel like you are finally home . . . and that, Janis, will be heaven."

"How do I get there Daddy?" "Don't worry, God knows the way, and so do you." "Will Mr. Phillips get there?" "I'm sure he'll get there too," Dad replied. "Are you sure Dad?" "Yes Janis, I'm sure."

We were almost home now. It was getting dark outside and we could see the kitchen lights on and Mother busy fixing dinner. I ran into the house and quickly forgot about our talk and our house call and Mr. Phillips. My life was filled with all the things of childhood—school and friends, studying, and growing up.

As the days passed I grew determined to study medicine and become a physician, just like my dad. I attended medical school and then did an internal medicine internship, a pathology residency, and a forensic pathology fellowship. I have begun to realize the profound effect my father's compassion had on me. I too began to listen to my patients and their loved ones and attempted to reassure them as my father had. As I listened, I learned more than I had ever imagined.

# PART II

# THE AWAKENING

Love is not just a force,
it is the mightiest force.

*Source unknown*

# PHYSICIAN, HEAL THYSELF

As a third-year medical student, I was required to take several 6-week rotations on the internal medicine service. I began to have patients of my own to examine, diagnose, and care for, all under the watchful eyes of the resident and staff physicians. My first rotation was at the Veterans Administration (VA) hospital in Minneapolis.

Back then, the old VA hospital was ringed by large, well-manicured lawns, which were studded with towering oak and elm trees that cast delightful shade in the summer and boasted beautiful gold, red, and rust colors in the fall. The hospital halls had gleaming, well-worn floors of marble, wood, and linoleum. The wards had the smell of old books mixed with the pungent odor of antiseptic.

I remember being proud of my new short white coat and the blue name tag announcing I was a medical student, and I tried to fling my stethoscope around my neck with the same casual abandon and confidence that I observed in the interns and residents. My new otoophthalmoscope (a gift from my father) and notebook were shoved deeply into the side pockets of my coat.

I walked down the long hall to 6AW, the "red medicine service," on that October Monday, all fresh, excited, and very nervous. The intern, Doug, introduced himself with a commanding manner: "Janis, welcome to red medicine. I expect you to work up the patients I assign you and care for them as your own. Don't expect a lot of extra help—I have 17 patients of my own. If you have questions, catch me or the staff doc. You can start by taking the next admit, some 66-year-old guy with a cough down in the ER (emergency room)—they are assigning him to me, and I am dumping him on you!"

I was a bit surprised at his tone, but in the spirit of showing no weakness, and as the only female medical student on 6AW, I answered, "No problem, I'll take care of it. Where can I find him? What is his name?"

"Mr. Larson, Don Larson," Doug shot over his shoulder as he charged off down the hall to catch the staff doctor.

I stood there, poised to act, thoughts racing through my head. "What should I do first? Which blood tubes to draw? The history and physical to do. How do I write 'orders'? Where is the ER? Where is my patient?"

The head nurse had evidently been watching me and must have seen the uncertainty. In a business-like but kind way, she directed me to the ward secretary and said, "Doctor, let me help you. I hear you are admitting Mr. Larson." She looked starched and capable. I felt grateful for her presence.

"Most everything you're going to need for pulling a chart together is located at the front desk area with the ward clerk. Needles, syringes, and blood tubes are located at the nurses' station," she offered as she gathered me up, introduced me to the nurses and clerk, and whisked me into the back rooms (the nuts and bolts areas) of 6AW.

"Thank you, thank you so much. I didn't know just where to begin," I answered as I grabbed papers for progress notes, order sheets, and request forms and stuffed red top, purple top, and blue top blood tubes in my coat pockets. "Ma'am?" I asked, "Could you tell me where the ER is—I mean, where my patient is?"

She was on to other things. "He is already on the floor, room 619 I believe." She gave me a reassuring smile and said, "Good luck!" as she hurried off.

I gathered up all the blood drawing supplies, the EKG (electrocardiogram) and the pulmonary function machines, and the forms for the chart, and walked briskly down the hall to room 619. I knocked on the open door. Mr. Larson was sitting on his bed, wearing a hospital gown, robe, and slippers. The bed was next to a big window in the 12-foot-high room. A ceiling fan was lazily circulating warm air. Sunlight was streaming in the window and lighting up the golden red leaves on the oak tree just outside. Mr. Larson was gazing intently out the window. I remember being struck by the calm in Mr. Larson's room—a sharp contrast from the bustle of the front desk.

"Good morning, Mr. Larson," I said. "I am Janis Amatuzio. I will be your primary doctor." He looked graciously at me as he extended his hand to meet mine. I felt somewhat self-conscious of my short white coat—the mark of a student doctor—so I hastily added, "I'm the third-year med student assigned to the red medicine service."

He could not have been kinder even though his skin looked a little gray and his eyes somewhat worried. "Very nice to meet you, Doctor."

I proceeded to explain that I would be doing a history and physical exam, drawing blood, and so on. He nodded and listened quietly. When I finished, a somewhat awkward moment followed. Finally, I just sat down on a chair next to his bed and said, "What's wrong?"

"I have a cough that just doesn't seem to go away, and I have been feeling more tired than usual. I suspect that I am ill. I'm a little worried about it."

"Oh, don't worry Mr. Larson," I answered quickly. "I'm sure we can figure this out. The chest X ray taken in the ER shows pneumonia on the right side—you know that may be the cause of your symptoms," I quickly said. "Do you smoke?" I asked. "Yes, but I quit 3 years ago. I started smoking when I was in the army. Almost a pack a day," he added. "What I must do right now," I explained, "is to ask a few more questions, do the physical examination, draw some blood, and perform a few routine tests," as I pointed to the EKG and pulmonary function test equipment.

As the sunlight spilled over us, and in the calm of room 619, I carefully listened to Mr. Larson's chest and abdomen, proceeded to make my assessments, and to order some tests.

In those times, the diagnostic wheels moved slowly. Over the next few days, as the test results came back, I noted abnormalities in Mr. Larson's blood work which, coupled with a history of slight weight loss, prompted me to obtain a consultation from the pulmonary specialists to further evaluate the pneumonia and antibiotic treatment. In the meantime, I found myself enjoying the daily visits with my patient, discovering that he had returned to farming after serving in World War II. He didn't speak much of the war. He had a keen appreciation for the land and he loved to talk about his crops and the weather. I suspected that the calmness and warmth that surrounded him sprang from a deeper wisdom and understanding of life and living.

The antibiotics seemed to be working and his cough had begun to subside. On that next Saturday morning, when I came in to make rounds with my intern and resident, Doug informed me that the pulmonary specialists had been asking for me that morning and wanted me down in the X-ray department. Mr. Larson had coughed up blood during the night. I checked in on him and found him lying quietly in bed, gazing out the window thoughtfully. His eyes met mine immediately and I could see that he seemed concerned. "I coughed up some blood last night. I'm afraid it really worried the nurses because that lung specialist, Dr. Tanheiser, came in to see me right away."

"I notice that he ordered another chest X ray on you," I answered.

"That's not all!" he exclaimed. "That doc insisted on looking down my wind pipe with a long tube. I darn near choked to death!"

"Oh my," I replied while beginning to form the reasons that the pulmonary specialists wanted to meet with me that morning. "I am so sorry this all happened to you, but we have to get some answers." I reassured him, "I am going to meet with Dr. Tanheiser this morning and review the test results. I will stop back up and see you after that."

Dr. Tanheiser was a fourth-year resident, tall, confident, and good looking. He had just finished a rotation as chief resident and seemed reassuring and knowledgeable. I met him in the consult room in the X-ray department where he was reviewing the radiographs from several patients. "Dr. T," I said, "I understand you evaluated my patient, Mr. Larson, last night after he started coughing up blood."

"Why yes I did, Janis. He is a pretty sick guy you know." I must have looked a little confused. "Here," he said putting up several X rays, "let me explain. The antibiotic you placed him on did begin to clear up the pneumonia, but it also allows us to see this large mass sitting around the bronchus. This is a tumor," he pointed to a large white mass on X ray, "which in all likelihood caused the pneumonia by plugging up the airway. I biopsied it when I was in there with the scope last night. It's probably cancerous; it seems to have started to erode into some of the blood vessels. The pathology report should be out this morning."

I sat there stunned. There was the tumor, plain as day, in black and white, as big as a golf ball, filling the right side of Mr. Larson's chest. "Dr. T, what do you think. . . ." He looked at me. "I mean what type of tumor do you think this is?"

"Oh," he answered quickly, "a malignant one. Look at these enlarged lymph nodes." He pointed to the nodular densities near the middle of the X ray. "These certainly look like metastases (spread) to me. I'd say, with his history of cigarette smoking, this guy is doomed. I mean, this doesn't look curable to me and with the apparent spread of the tumor, he's not a surgical candidate—but we'll have to wait for the path report."

"But what can we do about this tumor? What can my patient, Mr. Larson, do now?" I urgently inquired. He must have seen the dismay on my face. "How can I tell him that?!" I blurted out.

Dr. T. looked surprised. "Well," he laughed, "tell him not to buy any steel-belted radials for one thing; he won't live long enough to wear them out! No really—you need to check the path report and then tell your patient the results. I'll be happy to stop by on Monday and discuss with him the options for chemotherapy or radiation." He got up to leave. "Don't worry Dr. A., this gets easier with practice. Tell him: 'If you smoke, you get lung cancer.'" He left the room and strode down the hall.

My first patient had been in my care for only 5 days and, instead of recovering, was now about to be told that he was dying of lung cancer. "How can I do this," I thought. I gathered up my papers and ran quickly up to pathology where the chief resident was finishing up the morning slides with the staff pathologist, Dr. Jeski. Dr. Jeski was a lovely lady with slightly graying hair and a pleasant demeanor. I remembered her lectures from my second-year pathology class in medical school.

"Dr. Jeski, oh Dr. Jeski, could you please help me review a bronchial biopsy on my patient, Mr. Larson?"

Smiling, she said, "Well now Dr. Amatuzio, that's a step up—you finally have a patient! I'd be happy to review the biopsy with you. When was it taken?"

"Last night," I answered.

I proceeded to find the slide and request slip in the pathology office. The biopsy had already been read but the report had not yet been typed. I hurried into the staff office where Dr. Jeski patiently waited by the teaching microscope (it allowed three or four students or residents to view what the pathologist looked at). She took the slide, which had at least six small bits of tissue on it, all stained pink and purple, and confidently slipped it onto the stage (examining platform) and began to study these small pieces of Mr. Larson's lung. She moved the lenses quickly onto high power, then the room became very quiet as I, too, peered into the scope at the tissue. "Tell me," she said, "about your patient."

"Well, he is a 66-year-old farmer, World War II veteran, a cigarette smoker for 40 years, and father of four who came in for persistent right-sided pneumonia, which was confirmed by X ray. I started him on antibiotics 5 days ago. . . ."

She had moved the slide so that we were both peering at a disorganized, crowded group of cells with large, dark nuclei and irregular ugly shapes. I didn't like what I saw.

". . . as I said, 5 days ago, and we thought he was getting better, but yesterday he began to cough up blood and the pulmonary fellow was called in to see him. There is this big mass in the right chest now—one we couldn't see earlier. It was probably covered up by the pneumonia. We think it's a tumor. . . ."

"No, Janis, we know it's a tumor, and a highly malignant one at that. Look at these cells, all crowded together, pushing against one another, and invading into the adjacent tissue. This is cancer, probably poorly differentiated squamous cell carcinoma judging from some of these areas." She moved the biopsy slide quickly across the scope. "This man is in trouble—especially if this has already spread as I suspect it has."

I sat there at the scope. Dr. Jeski 's eyes met mine across the eye pieces. "I'm sorry," she said quietly.

In my mind's eye, Mr. Larson's finely lined face and kind eyes filled the room. "How will I tell him?" I blurted out. "What will I tell him? Oh Dr. Jeski, I've never done this before." Time seemed to stand still again. Dr. Jeski's gray hair was backlit by the sunlight coming through the windows.

"Janis, this wasn't taught to you in medical school was it?" I silently shook my head no. "You tell him in person, as gently, honestly, and clearly as you can. That is what he came here to learn, so that he can make some choices about his life, so that he can continue to live until he dies, just like the rest of us." She put her hand on my shoulder. "You know, Janis, I suspect he already knows. You will do just fine. Go now and talk to your patient."

I felt so grateful for Dr. Jeski's wisdom. Talking with her had calmed me. So I gathered up courage and walked back upstairs, down the long hallway to room 619. I paused outside his door and took a deep breath. I could see him lying on his bed, eyes turned toward the windows. He must be thinking about his farm and his family, I thought.

He looked pleased to see me when I walked in and he sat up, swinging his feet over the side. The bed next to his was unoccupied so I sat down there, smiled at him, and asked, "How are you feeling?"

"A little better. No more blood today," he proudly answered. And then his eyes began to study mine.

"I have something to tell you. I have the results of some of your tests."

What happened next I cannot explain, except to say while it was not one of my most professional moments, it was perhaps one of my most honest. As I looked at my patient's kind but worried eyes, the slight pallor of his skin, I couldn't help but feel the tears well up in my eyes. I fought them back and looked down.

"What's wrong Doctor?" he gently asked.

"You have lung cancer Mr. Larson, and I am so sorry," I responded. Then with no further thought, the tears rolled down my cheeks and I put my hands up to my face. I could not stop them, and I felt so terribly embarrassed. The next thing I knew, and much to my surprise, I felt Mr. Larson's arm around my shoulders as he moved over and sat down next to me on the bed. I looked over at him and noticed the tears streaming down his face as well. I put my arm around his shoulder as well. There we sat. The doctor and the patient. And we wept.

Then Mr. Larson, in his calm and knowing way, began to comfort me with his words. "You know, Janis, I suspected something was wrong. I've felt this way for 2 or 3 months. I am not surprised and, you know, I've sort of been planning for it."

"You have! How could you know?" I quickly asked.

He held up his hand. "I just knew it, and Janis," he looked at me, "it's okay. I'm okay."

"Mr. Larson, you don't understand, you're not okay. This is a big tumor. I suspect it has spread, and we need to do more tests to figure this out. Then we need to decide on the treatment. . . ."

He stopped me. "Dr. Amatuzio, I think you don't understand, so listen to me now." He got up from his bed and grabbed some tissues for me, and then sat down in an old rocking chair near the head of the bed. "I'm not going to have any more tests or any treatment. I'm going home." He paused and then said, "I feel more alive now than I ever have. I am so aware of all the love that surrounds me. I have a lovely wife—she is my best friend and has been my closest companion over the many years we've been together and I miss her." With a twinkle in his eye and patting his stomach, he added, "And she is a marvelous cook. I love sitting in my big rocking chair at home, and I love lying next to her in bed and holding her tight. I am going to enjoy my children and grandchildren and friends for as long as I can. And . . . it's fall, and I love the smell of the earth, harvesting my crops, and walking in my fields."

He paused, and once again stared out the window. The

shadows were lengthening in the late afternoon autumn sun. I profoundly felt that in this moment, I was the student in the presence of great wisdom, clear and focused by the day's unfolding events—wisdom that I dearly needed. We talked into the early evening. Mr. Larson made plans to leave the next morning and continue his care at home. When I finally got up to go, I hugged him and thanked him for being my first patient, and again apologized for crying.

"Janis, I have all the love I'll ever need and that includes yours. Thank you for being my doctor."

I drove home that evening awash in emotions. I felt embarrassed that I had cried and wondered if I had done enough to persuade him to stay and try treatment. I began to second guess myself, and in some strange way, felt like I had failed. My medical training had prepared me for action, to diagnose and treat, to save lives and push the limits with medication, chemotherapy, radiation therapy, and surgery . . . for anything except going home!!

I never told anyone that I had cried in Mr. Larson's room, and I proceeded through the rest of my clinical rotations determined to keep all of my patients alive with all the skill I possessed.

Mr. Larson was all right with his decision, but I certainly wasn't.

I realize now that I did not have the wisdom to distinguish the enormous difference between "giving up" and "letting go." The first seems to come from despair, the other from acceptance and wisdom drawn from thoughtful living and deliberate awareness. At that point of my learning, it was much easier to try to master disease than to attempt to understand the mysteries of living and dying.

The day I received a thank-you card from the Larson family, I cried again. My first patient had died at home after Christmas in the arms of his wife and in the loving presence of his family. He was buried near his beloved farm.

I didn't know that medicine would be so hard. I had much to learn.

# "UNTIL THE TWELFTH OF NEVER"

I started my internal medicine internship at the University Hospitals ahead of schedule, taking the place of a resident who had dropped out. The hours were long and the pace was grueling; nothing had prepared me for being so tired for so long. One problem with starting my internship early was that all the other interns were much more experienced, and consequently faster—it seemed they were infinitely more confident. But even through the haze of the fatigue, I felt close to the pulse of the hospital and the heart of its patients.

I rotated onto 5B at the VA hospital, a familiar place from medical school days. I even remembered several of the nurses. My second night on call was a Saturday, and I took nine "hits" from the ER. The patients were very sick. Two went directly to the intensive care unit—one with a bleeding ulcer and the other with an acute heart attack. A third I transferred to the surgical service with what proved to be a ruptured appendix. The other patients I worked up one by one, doing their histories and physicals and ordering laboratory tests. Unfortunately, by the time I got to the ninth patient, it was after 2:30 in the morning. I walked down the now darkened hallway, the silence broken only by occasional snores, wheeling the spirometer and the EKG machine with me. Room 528 was dark, the door halfway open. I stopped to check the chart the nurse had given me—just to be sure I had the right room. "Mr. Gunnar, Room 528, Recurrent lymphoma" was written across the top.

I paused, sorry that I had to awaken my patient. "Better late than never," I thought. I knocked softly as I entered the room. "Mr. Gunnar, I'm Dr. Amatuzio. I'm sorry it's so late. I have to talk with you and examine you." He must have been sleeping only lightly because he immediately awakened, turned on the light, and sat up in bed.

Even in the dim light of the bedside lamp, he looked a little jaundiced and pale to me. "Mr. Gunnar," I said as I pulled a chair closer to his bed, "let's talk a little first. Tell me about yourself and why you came to the ER tonight."

He cleared his throat. "Well as you probably know, I was diagnosed with lymphoma 2 years ago." He pulled up his hospital gown and pointed to the healed scar on his abdomen that looked like a giant zipper. "They went in and took all sorts of biopsies back then, and even took my spleen out. I was started on chemotherapy and lost all my hair, but I got better and went into remission. I even went back to work."

"What kind of work do you do?" I asked.

"I'm an accountant," he answered. "I work with two other guys. We have a small business together. I also analyze handwriting on the side," he added with a smile.

"I'd like to learn about that," I said smiling.

"But, go on," I urged.

"About 6 months later, my doctor told me the lymphoma cells had gotten into my blood stream, so more chemotherapy followed. I was doing well for nearly a year until about 4 weeks ago when I started to get very tired. I don't know, maybe I was pushing too hard. My son just got married and I was helping him with his new house—and we put up a garage!"

"My, what a wonderful thing for you to do."

"I know," he smiled and replied, "so I rested up . . . but Doc, the fatigue just won't go away, and the night before last I started to look a little yellow in my eyeballs. My dear wife, Maggie, insisted that I come in tonight. It probably could have waited until morning, but she worries about me a lot," he humbly finished.

I put my hand on his wrist. His skin was warm and dry, but his pulse seemed a little faster than I had expected—100-110 beats per minute at rest. I was worried. "Have you had any abdominal pain or difficulty after eating a meal?" I asked, hoping against hope that his jaundice might be related to the gallbladder or biliary tract disease.

"No, Doc. In fact, I don't have much appetite at all. I feel sick but I can't put my finger on what's really wrong."

I proceeded with the rest of the history review and examined him. "Have you lost any weight lately?"

"Yes, a few pounds, not much," he answered.

I drew Mr. Gunnar's blood and decided that I would review the smears myself yet that night. It was now 3:40 AM. I told Mr. Gunnar that he should get some sleep and that I would check back with him in the morning.

"Thank you, Doc," he said.

As I turned to leave, he called out, "But one more thing." I stopped and came back to the edge of his bed. "Uh, . . . my wife, Maggie—she is so worried. You know, tomorrow is my birthday. Please don't say anything to her without me."

"Mr. Gunnar, I promise you this: I will talk with both of you together. No secrets."

He paused and sighed, "Thank you."

"Good night now."

"Good night," he replied.

I had a sense of foreboding and urgency as I walked back down the corridor towards the small clinical laboratory in the chief resident's office. This was set up so the interns could spin a hematocrit (an estimate of the number of red blood cells) and do a preliminary white blood count with differential, but the initial lab results were always confirmed by the main laboratory. An old gray A&O microscope with an intermittent light source and worn lenses sat on a small table next to the wall. I put the capillary tube in the centrifuge for the hematocrit and hastily made a blood smear on a glass slide and stained it. While waiting for the centrifuge to complete its spinning, I walked down the quiet hall to the pop machine and got myself a Diet Coke, thinking, "What a long night."

When I returned with Coke in hand, the centrifuge had come to a stop. The spun hematocrit was only 18 mm (normal being 36-40), indicating a very low hemoglobin. The glass slide was ready, stained a deep purple and still wet when I slipped it onto the microscope. Mr. Gunnar's red blood cells seemed dwarfed by large unusual white blood cells, unlike anything that I had seen before, and far too numerous to count. Leukemia, I thought. But they didn't look like any leukemic cells I remembered from my med school hematology classes. I peered at them moving from field to field—they were simultaneously fascinating and horrible.

I lost track of time sitting there at the scope. Before I knew it, it was dawn. The sky was growing pale pink on the horizon. Mr. Gunnar needed a blood transfusion, but more importantly, he needed a diagnosis. I took the smear, put it into my pocket, and quickly headed down the hall to the women's locker room for a hot shower and change of clothes before the day began all over again.

The resident in charge of the "blue medicine service," the one I reported to, usually arrived by 6:30 AM. I was determined to see him to discuss Mr. Gunnar's symptoms and peripheral smear, and also requested a medical consultation from the hematology–oncology (Hem–Onc) service.

The time flew by—a blur of rounds, charts, and laboratory results. Late morning, as we continued our rounds, out of the corner of my eye I saw the Hem–Onc chief resident come striding down the corridor in his white coat, medical students trailing behind him. "Richter's Syndrome" he announced. "It is Richter's Syndrome." (I remember thinking that I didn't have a clue about Richter's Syndrome. I wasn't even sure I had even heard the term before.) "John Gunnar has Richter's Syndrome," he proclaimed.

"It's an unusual complication of chronic lymphocytic

leukemia—it's also known as a 'blast crisis'" he said. "In other words, the bone marrow floods the blood stream with very young, immature leukemic cells . . . very unusual case. It can be fatal very rapidly without aggressive chemotherapy. It usually signifies the beginning of a rough clinical course."

He asked me, "How high is the white count this morning?"

I flipped rapidly through the chart—"92,000 with 80 percent immature 'blasts,' hemoglobin 6.2, platelets 55,000," I rattled off.

"Whew. He needs a bone marrow biopsy stat. Then we need to make some treatment decisions. Order blood for a type and cross for four units of packed cells. What are his blood clotting tests?"

"His protime is 16 seconds with a control time of 12.5 seconds. I haven't done a bleeding time," I replied.

"Better hang a unit of fresh frozen plasma before you start the marrow—but do it quick," he ordered. "I'll be back right after lunch and we will review the aspirate of the marrow together down in 'special heme.'" He turned and strode back down the hall, white coat and students streaming behind him.

As he turned, I noticed a woman standing at the door of Mr. Gunnar's room. Her troubled eyes met mine only briefly before she looked down at the floor. She had slightly graying blond hair and was holding her coat over her arm. She quickly slipped into Mr. Gunnar's room. I was pretty sure she had heard what we had been discussing. "I had better go talk with Mr. Gunnar about this," I told my resident.

"No," he answered. "Go get the bone marrow tray, a consent form, and call the lab to order up the fresh frozen plasma and the type and cross for the packed red blood cells. Then we'll go talk to him together."

When I returned, my resident was already in the room. As I had thought, the pale blond woman was Maggie, Mr. Gunnar's wife. I introduced myself quietly. Mr. Gunnar was sitting up in bed as my resident explained the lab work, the white blood count, and the need to perform a bone marrow biopsy.

"What does this mean?" Mrs. Gunnar asked, a little bewildered.

"That your husband's disease has taken a new twist. He is a very sick man." He continued, "I can't say much more until we get the test results back."

Mr. Gunnar had been listening very intently and stated, "Well, let's get it over with. I've had one of these procedures before." Mr. Gunnar locked his eyes on his wife, and, with the quiet dignity and strength that I came to expect of him, said, "Sit down here next to me, Maggie, and hold my hand." His truly take-charge attitude steadied not only his wife, but all of us. I remember thinking that I understood better the meaning of courage—as Ernest Hemingway put it, "grace under pressure."

The day's events unfolded. Mr. Gunnar's bone marrow exam showed, unfortunately, that the malignant cells (blasts) had nearly replaced his normal bone marrow cells. With his consent, we launched into the only course open to him— aggressive chemotherapy. His only chance was to try to knock out the leukemic cells. Unfortunately, the therapy also destroyed the other white blood cells, those which fought off infection.

His clinical course was turbulent. His body wracked with violent episodes of nausea and profound fatigue and weakness. But he never faltered in his decision to try for a cure. As the chemotherapy progressed, he developed pneumonia and then sepsis, which were treated with intravenous antibiotics.

I checked his blood counts daily, watching closely for the return of healthy noncancerous white blood cells.

Mr. Gunnar slept much of the time and, over the next few weeks, I began to enjoy my visits with his wife, an English teacher, who faithfully kept vigil at his bedside, frequently holding his hand. She always inquired about his white count and platelets. When I stopped one late afternoon, she got up out of her rocker and inquired, "Doctor, do you think he can hear me?"

"What do you mean?" I asked.

"Well," she replied, "He seems to be sleeping so much and when he is awake, he is hardly conscious. We've always enjoyed reading poetry to one another. . . . I would like to read some to him now."

I looked at Mr. Gunnar, barely arousable, his body hooked up to two IV (intravenous) catheters, and the hair on his head gone from the chemotherapy. The chemotherapy and infections had taken their toll. His body was struggling to revive. "Go ahead, read to him. I think— just maybe—he will hear you." She smiled and thanked me and sat back down in the rocking chair. I left the room, thinking again that not much in medical school had prepared me for this.

Later that evening, as I made my rounds, I found Mrs. Gunnar asleep in the chair next to her husband's bed. On her lap was an open book of poetry with that most passionate poem Elizabeth Barrett Browning had written to her husband, Robert Browning, on love in "Sonnets from the Portuguese."

"How do I love thee, let me count the ways.
I love thee. . . ."
And tears filled my eyes.

Mr. Gunnar courageously clung to life. The chemotherapy had done its work and now we waited patiently for his bone marrow to recover. Because of his compromised immune system, he wasn't allowed many visitors. However, his room was filled with cards from family and friends.

After a rare weekend off, I returned to the blue medicine service. Mr. Gunnar's bone-marrow had not yet improved—and we were all becoming anxious. Maggie kept her faithful vigil and daily read out loud her favorite poems. I'll never forget that evening, as I was walking down the hall of 5A West, I heard the unmistakable sound of music coming from #527—Mr. Gunnar's room. I slowed down near the door and stood in the hall and listened. It was a strangely beautiful melody . . . it was Johnny Mathis singing:

"I'll love you till the roses forget to bloom.
I'll love you till the flowers have lost their perfume.
I'll love you till the bluebirds forget to sing.
Until the twelfth of never, I'll still be loving you.
Hold me tight, never let me go, hold me close.
Fill my heart with. . . ."

Mrs. Gunnar had brought in a record player. She was there, sitting next to him and rubbing his back. I just kept walking and thought, "What a grand love they share!"

"He just has to be better," I thought. That evening the lab results showed that the white blood count had dipped to slightly less than 500. I was worried, and after consulting with the hematology specialist, decided to start him on a new experimental medication that just might help stimulate the marrow to begin making new white and red blood cells. I went into his room and explained the new medication. I also carefully listened to his lungs and abdomen. There was no sign of infection or fever. But I cautioned the nurses to watch him closely. I wasn't going to lose this patient, not for me or for Maggie!

Mrs. Gunnar must have seen the look of concern in my eyes when I told her the white blood cell counts had slightly decreased. "What does that mean?" she asked.

"Well, it could be nothing at all, really, but sometimes it means the onset of an infection. But," I said quickly, holding up my hand, "I don't see any signs whatsoever right now, and we are watching closely. I started him on a new medication designed to help stimulate the marrow. It's a long shot, but I think we should try it. The nurses will be checking his pulse, blood pressure, and temperature every 2 hours throughout the night."

"I'm planning to spend the night here," she said. "I want to be close by." There was a small couch in the room that made into a day bed. Maggie had spent several nights there before.

I was off call that night and planned to go after checking Mr. Gunnar one more time and leaving orders with the nurses to call me if there was any change.

He was lying peacefully in bed and aroused when I walked in. Maggie excused herself, and stepped out into the hall. "I've asked the nurses to check on you every 2 hours." Then I paused and sat down in the chair beside the bed. "How are you doing, really?" I asked.

"Doc, I am really fine," he said. "I'm just a little tired out, that's all."

"I know," I answered.

"I've had quite a few visitors today."

"Visitors?" I asked. Mr. Gunnar had closed his eyes and didn't answer me. Strict orders had been given to restrict visitors to immediate family only, because of the risk of infection. My mind was whirling. No wonder the counts had dropped—he had been exposed to a new bacteria or virus, I feared.

"Mr. Gunnar, who stopped in to visit you? You know that you're not supposed to. . . ."

"Don't worry, Doc," he interrupted. "They were some folks I hadn't seen in a long time, my older brother and his friend. We had a nice talk, caught up on some things." He paused. "The truth is, I've never been better. Don't worry about me, I'll be just fine."

He opened up his eyes and looked right at me. "Go home now. I need some rest and so do you." That was just like Mr. Gunnar, always looking out for someone else, even when he was desperately ill.

When I came back to work the next morning, Mr. Gunnar 's room was empty: the sheets were stripped from the bed, the cards were gone from the door. The charge nurse saw me standing there and walked up behind me. "Your patient died in his sleep last night. His dear wife was at his side. She didn't want an autopsy."

"What!!!" I exclaimed.

"He died in his sleep."

"You didn't call me?" My heart was beating wildly, and I felt the blood rising to my cheeks. "I left orders to call me if anything happened."

"We had the house doctor come up and pronounce

him. There wasn't anything that anyone else could do!" she said quickly.

"Did you have any indication that there was anything wrong . . . did he become feverish, or. . . ."

"No, Doctor. We were checking him every 2 hours. His blood pressure and pulse were steady and his temperature was normal. His wife fell asleep in the bed next to him about midnight, so we didn't disturb her. When we went in to check him at a little after 1:00 AM, he was dead. There was no pulse, no respirations, nothing."

I was stunned. I just couldn't believe it. What's more, I was furious that my patient had died.

"Thank you," I said and took a deep breath. I stood there for a moment, then walked into his room and sat down in the chair. Tears filled my eyes. I realized that I didn't have a chance to say goodbye. The room, which seemed so empty yet bright, was filled with the smell of fresh antiseptic. Sitting there, I remembered Mr. Gunnar, his courage, his wife, and I felt privileged to have glimpsed the passion of the grand love that bound him and Maggie . . . and bereft that I hadn't kept him alive.

Just then, my pager went off. Another "hit" from the ER. I was admitting patients that day and there was no time to waste. I quickly grabbed their address from the chart. "I'll send Maggie a card," I vowed.

Several weeks later, I received a call from Maggie at work. She thanked me for being her husband's doctor and for caring for him.

"What happened that night?" I asked her.

"He just slipped away while I was sleeping. I couldn't have been any closer," she said. "I remember that we kissed goodnight."

"I'm so sorry," I said.

"His death was such a surprise, but you know, he really had such a good day."

"Well, it must have been nice for him to visit with his brother and his friend. He told me that they stopped in to see him."

There was a long pause on the line. "What?" she said.

"His brother and his friend stopped by to visit. I was a little concerned because he wasn't supposed to have anyone except immediate family."

"Doctor," she said, her voice strained. "My husband had only one brother and he and his best friend were killed in an accident over 40 years ago."

Now it was my turn to pause. "Maybe it was the new medication we started him on," I said. "Or maybe. . . ."

"Or maybe they are all together now. Thank you for telling me," she said. "The most important thing to me now is that we had each other. It's enough."

I hung up the phone after we said goodbye. I searched my memory. I was sure of what Mr. Gunnar had told me that last evening. It was all very strange.

# FIRST LIGHT

You know, Doc, . . . I died once. . . ."

It was 3:00 AM. The light above my patient's bed formed
a perfect cone of light over us as I attempted to restart his
IV catheter for heparin therapy. I was in the last month of
my internal medicine internship and doing a rotation in the
heart hospital—where we worked a grueling 36 hours and
were off 12. The nurse had hot-packed my patient's arm to
make his veins more pronounced. I had just gotten to bed
30 minutes earlier when Mr. Stein's IV catheter dislodged.
The nurse awakened me with an apology.

As I sat on the chair next to his bed, I remember thinking
how tired I was, and that this man must be out of his mind.
"Really?" I answered, still searching for a vein.

His face looked swollen but his eyes were bright and clear.
"I know you don't believe me, Doctor," he paused. "I'm sorry
that you had to get up. . . ."

My heart went out to him as I reached out and took his hand.

"It's okay Mr. Stein. It's important for you to have this medication." The skin of his left arm was swollen and taut, and even though it was moist and warm, finding a vein was difficult.

"Blood clots like to form in my legs and travel up to my lungs. The doctors think I have some clots in my legs now," he said.

"Yes," I replied, "that's why it's so important that you get this medication into your veins."

"Two years ago they put a filter, a screen, in my abdomen, in the inferior vena cava, to stop the clots from passing to my lungs. That's when I died."

Finally, palpating what seemed like a promising vein, I nodded and countered with, "But you're here now."

"Yes," he said, "I came back to life."

For no good reason, I felt a shiver go down my back.

"What happened to you?" As unbelievable as it had seemed at first, I felt intrigued.

"Well, the doctors had just finished the surgery, which took about 5 hours. I awoke in the post-anesthesia recovery room and the nurses told me that it had gone well. But I remember having difficulty staying awake—the nurse kept squeezing my shoulder."

"Go on," I urged. My curiosity was aroused by his story. The heparin access was now securely taped to his arm.

"It was the strangest thing that has ever happened to me, Doctor. All of a sudden I left my body, right through the top of my head! I found myself looking down on me—I mean on my body—from the ceiling. I felt so sorry for my body. Suddenly, the doctors and nurses came rushing to my side and began resuscitation. I was puzzled because I was just fine. I could feel their concern and, what's more, I could read their thoughts. I went to the doctor's side and tapped him on the shoulder. He didn't feel me, so I got right in front of him and said, 'Stop all of that, I'm fine!' He didn't hear me, but I could "hear" every thought he had. One of the nurses was upset that she had to stay and help. I knew her thoughts. She was looking forward to a date right after work!!"

"You mean that you could read every thought they had?" I asked.

"Yes, it's strange but it was almost like feeling every thought—like reading their minds!!"

"That's incredible," I said. "What did you do then?"

"I watched them working furiously on my body. They were using shock paddles—my body jumped every time they were used. Then, the man in the bed next to me had a cardiac arrest."

"How do you know that?"

"I watched it—the whole thing. His heart stopped pumping and he left his body, too, right through the top of his head. And did he ever look surprised to see me! I communicated with him by just thinking and told him what had happened."

Amazed at what I was hearing, and glad no one would interrupt us at this time of the morning, I urged him to continue. "What happened next?"

"We watched the confusion below us from some spot up near the ceiling. There was only one emergency cart and the doctor was shouting orders and calling for help. The shock paddles were on the emergency cart and the poor doctor would shock one body and then turn around and shock the other. There weren't enough supplies, because so much had already been used on me."

"So what did you do then?"

"Well, when it became clear to us that we couldn't communicate with them, and, you know, it seemed odd, but I didn't feel attached to my body, so we both left the room."

"How did you do that?" I asked. "Did you go through the doors into the hallway? I mean, how did you move?"

"Well," he said, "this sounds strange again, but we just 'thought' our way over to the hallway—and we didn't go through the doors, we went right through the walls. I remember seeing the waiting room near the operating room. There were still several people there and I could feel their concern for the well-being of their loved ones. Then we moved on."

"To where?" I again inquired.

"We left the building . . . we went right through the wall. I remember looking back at the red brick and mortar. And then we were outside. All was calm and still, but it seemed different, somehow warm, and then I saw it. . . ." Mr. Stein's voice trailed off.

"Saw what?" I prompted.

"Off in the distance I saw—no I felt—the most amazingly beautiful Light. It was so bright, it was made up of every color of the rainbow and more. I was instantly drawn to it and so was my companion. As we approached this dazzling Light, I felt the most incredible joy and awe and sense of grandeur I've ever experienced—words don't do it justice. Then the Light opened up into a cone or tunnel. I felt a rush as I moved through it. There were the most incredible colors there—some I had never seen before or since. I saw my mother and father, my dear aunt, and my dog. They were smiling at me and it seemed like a joyful reunion, a celebration. I was filled with such happiness and anticipation. As I traveled upward toward the source of all this joy, I grew more aware. The brilliant, dazzling colors shimmered, and I began to realize . . . well . . . everything. I can't explain it. All at once, I remembered the purpose of my life. I understood how it all worked. I realized that it was all, somehow, perfect. I was overwhelmed and stunned by the loving kindness that surrounded me.

"I was still aware of my companion, he continued to accompany me. Suddenly, I realized—or maybe it became clear—that I could not stay, that I must return to my body. In that instant, I knew with crystal clarity the reasons why. And, you know, my companion, the other man who left the recovery room with me?"

"Yes?"

"Well, . . ." he paused momentarily, looking a little sad. "He got to go toward that dazzling Light. I had to come back."

We just sat there. Tears were streaming down his face onto his chest, but his eyes remained bright. "I have never told that entire story to anyone before," Mr. Stein confided.

"Thank you for telling me," I replied softly.

We continued to sit there for awhile in the silence, Mr. Stein added, "The next thing I knew, I was back in my body. Everything hurt. I felt sick and I was tired, and I hurt all over. But I was also amazed—amazed at what had just happened to me. Most of all, I remember the incredible peacefulness. It seemed as though, truly, nothing mattered. I was so overwhelmed that I just kept it all to myself and kept trying to remember all that happened.

"The next day, my doctor told me what had transpired in the recovery room—that I had had a heart attack and that they had almost 'lost' me. Approximately a month later at one of my check-up visits, I decided to tell my doctor about this experience. I was still overcome by the immense sense of purpose and peacefulness I now felt. I jumped right in, telling him how I had left my body and floated up in the air near the ceiling, how I could read every thought, and about the wonderful Light. I could see that he looked confused with disbelief. 'You must have had an unusual reaction to the anesthetic medication,' he said. 'No it wasn't a reaction,' I claimed, 'it was the most real thing that has ever happened to me.' Then the doctor said, 'Listen here, you don't know what you are saying. You were dead, dead and gone. We attempted resuscitation for over 15 minutes. Your heart was not pumping! Then, bango, your heart started again . . . and here you are. Alive and recovering.'

"'Doctor,' I told him, 'I watched you during that incredible resuscitation.' To which he stated, 'Impossible—you were unconscious.' So I told him, 'Well, I saw that the man in the bed next to me died too . . . and that you only had one emergency cart and one set of defibrillation paddles and that there weren't enough medications and how you moved back and forth between his bed and mine. I felt how worried, frustrated, and concerned you and the staff were. . . .'

"The doctor just looked puzzled, paused, and then said, 'You could not have known that; someone must have told you. I can't believe this,' he said shaking his head. Then holding up his hand added, 'I don't know what you believe happened, but for all intents and purposes, you were dead.' 'I know,' I answered.

"Well," he continued, "we never spoke of that experience again. In fact, I felt embarrassed and even doubted it for awhile—but I have never forgotten it and, in my heart, I know that it happened."

It was almost 4:00 AM. I sat there for a few more minutes. I felt that the moment and the story were extraordinary. "Has this changed your life?" I asked.

"Oh yes," Mr. Stein said thoughtfully, "in several ways. First, I don't fear death at all. I know that we do not die. The experience that I had called 'dying' was the most magnificent thing that has ever happened to me. Secondly, I know that love is really all that counts, and that it is of no consequence to store up or value material things. It is who we are being that matters. And lastly, I try to learn something each day—to gather knowledge and then try to apply it to make this world, my world, a better place."

I thanked Mr. Stein and told him that I believed him and the incredible journey he had taken. I was sure that his experience of joy and understanding would last a lifetime. And, more than anything else, I hoped and dreamed and dared to believe that what he said was the truth.

This experience was something I too held in my heart for weeks, months, and years. When I would be tempted to dismiss it, I would remember that this experience had changed Mr. Stein's life . . . and I began to use the simple but profound wisdom he had shared.

# PART III
# SPEAKING FOR THE DEAD

The most beautiful thing we can experience
is the mysterious.

*Albert Einstein*

# FORENSIC PATHOLOGY: THE EXAMINATION OF A LIFE

In 1978, the spring of my internship year, I was accepted into a pathology residency that would include 4 years of study in anatomic and clinical pathology and a year of training in forensic pathology at the highly acclaimed Hennepin County Medical Examiner's Office. Following this training, I practiced forensic pathology in Hastings, Minnesota, and served as assistant coroner for several southern Minnesota counties. In 1993, I was appointed coroner for Anoka County and, subsequently, for several nearby jursidictions.

Death investigation is really the examination of a life. It's an effort to learn everything possible about how a person lived and died. After death, all the investigator can rely on are clues, telltale signs, and observations. The scene of the death gives an enormous amount of information about the person and their habits. The position of the body, the state of clothing, and the postmortem signs of rigor, livor, and algor can help tell the investigator about the time elapsed since death and whether the body was moved or was in a struggle. The circumstances of the death are essential to the investigation, including medical conditions, social situations, and a knowledge of the events immediately prior to death. These facts are usually gained from those who know the person best—family, friends, physicians, and sometimes neighbors. In other words, the investigator has to ask the right questions and listen for the answers. The "rest of the story" is usually discovered at the autopsy.

When a death occurs under "unnatural circumstances," such as an apparent accident, suicide, or homicide, or suddenly and unexpectedly in a young person, a postmortem examination (autopsy) is usually performed as part of the investigative process. In most jurisdictions, family members are informed of the decision to autopsy. Their concerns and beliefs are taken into account because an autopsy is such an "intimate" procedure.

In forensic pathology, talking with family members is essential to uncovering the clues about circumstances that can otherwise seem baffling to the investigator. Besides the initial contacts, I have made it a practice on noncriminal cases to call family members after the scene investigation and autopsy to explain the preliminary findings and what appeared to have happened. These conversations and meetings are the source of the rich experiences that follow.

# THE KISS GOODBYE

Notifying the next of kin about the death of their loved one is a daunting task for the investigator—one that doesn't get easier with practice. It should be done clearly, kindly, and always in person. Not surprisingly, the notification that stands out most clearly in my mind was my first.

It was a cloudless, sunny July day, and already hot by 9:00 AM. The coroner's office was notified of a death at an industrial job site. It was my first week, and being the forensic fellow, I jumped at the opportunity to accompany the investigators to the scene. We climbed into the specially equipped medical examiner's rig, stocked with body bags, gloves, gowns, film, and evidence collection kits, and headed out to the scene. The death had occurred at a newly constructed business park. Crews were busy placing sewer pipes and building roads.

We found our way through the maze of the construction equipment to the place where police had cordoned off an area around a large dump truck and front end loader. There were many squad cars present with flashing lights, as well as a fire truck and ambulance. I noticed the firefighters sweating profusely in their heavy coveralls and the EMTs (emergency medical technicians) and police officers all standing around . . . these men and women so prepared for and accustomed to lightening-quick action, now stopped, pausing, waiting, and watching. As we pulled up, I noticed that the construction site was unusually quiet, and I had the feeling that they were waiting for more than us—perhaps for an answer, a reason why a young construction worker had lost his life senselessly and accidentally that morning.

Tom Smith, the investigator on duty, confidently swung into action, with both the investigative assistant and me trailing behind. Tom obtained the history from the officer in charge and the construction boss. The dead man was identified by his coworkers. He and his pipe-fitting crew had just stopped for their morning break. The site was usually noisy. A large industrial dump truck had begun backing up, and its audible backup warning system failed to sound. The right rear tire had crushed the decedent's upper body as he sat on the ground. The body was covered with a blanket; his coworkers were standing protectively close. I watched as the photos and measurements were taken. The body was examined, a blanket was held up to shield it from plain view and Tom removed the wallet, wristwatch, and wedding ring. The man's identification by coworkers would later be confirmed by comparing dental records. The remains were placed into a body bag and carefully loaded in the back of our van. An autopsy was indicated, and OSHA (Occupational Safety and Health Administration) would be notified. But a more pressing issue was waiting—notification of the decedent's wife.

Tom asked a Minneapolis police officer to accompany us as we proceeded into a modest but well-kept neighborhood in northeast Minneapolis. The stares from the people on the sidewalks and front lawns confirmed the gravity of our task.

We pulled up to a small white house with white taffeta curtains blowing through the partly opened front windows. As we walked up the front sidewalk, I felt myself wanting to hide behind Mr. Smith's large frame. The officer knocked on the front door and we waited. The door slowly opened and a lovely young woman, dressed in nightgown and housecoat, with light brown hair spilling over her shoulders, greeted us with concerned blue eyes.

"Mrs. Brown?" Mr. Smith asked.

"Yes, I'm Mrs. Brown," she answered.

"Ma'am, I'm Mr. Smith from the medical examiner's

office. Your husband was killed this morning in a construction accident."

Her eyes widened and filled with tears, as she put her
hand to her mouth and said, "Oh, thank God I kissed him
goodbye!" She then collapsed into the officer's arms,
awash with tears and grief. My heart was torn in half that
morning too as I watched and learned—but I never forgot
her words.

In that moment I realized more fully the impact of the
work I had chosen for a career. I felt on a gut level everything
that I had taken for granted. It came to me with absolute
clarity that today could be the last day for someone that I
dearly loved, or it could be my own. I felt as if I had been a
sleepwalker suddenly jolted awake.

❧

I have recounted the story of that day's events many times
to friends, coworkers, and family over the past years. The
story still carries the same impact for me as it did the first
day I heard it.

Several months ago, I sent a sympathy card to a friend of
mine, a county attorney, whose father had died after a long
illness. I received a beautiful letter from him in return.

*Janis,*

*At my father's death, I was reminded of a story you told me about the young woman who just received news of her husband's fatal accident. "Thank God I kissed him goodbye" was her reaction to the news. I have never forgotten that story. My family and I got the chance to say goodbye to my father as he was in hospice for the final 5 days. I never understood that concept until now. While there is grief over my father's death, there is no tragedy. You see death many times and many ways and the resultant family reactions. My father was lucky enough to die in a beautiful setting with my mother holding his hand. Unlike that young woman, we had the chance to say goodbye. We have loss but we also have peace knowing that he wanted to "go home," as he said just before he died. When a parent dies, part of you dies but a part of you grows up a little more, too. Thank you for your thoughts.*

[A.C.P., used with permission]

That young widow gave me a great gift. I wondered how different the world would be if we each remembered to treat one another as if each encounter might be our last. But most of all, I remembered to kiss my loved ones goodbye.

# I KNOW THE SECRET

On rare occasions, family members will ask to see the bodies of their loved ones in the morgue—a practice I tend to discourage. The county morgue is a busy place, and although clean and tidy, has a distinct laboratory atmosphere not befitting final goodbyes.

One slippery, snowy March day in 1993, a 44-year-old woman who was driving her car to work was struck on the passenger side by a pickup truck that skidded through a stop sign. Though wearing a seat belt, she was critically injured and rushed to the emergency room—where resuscitative efforts failed.

The decedent, Judy, had never married and her mother was listed as her closest relative. The ER staff had notified Judy's mother of the accident and the critical nature of the injuries. She had rushed to the hospital only to find that her daughter had been pronounced dead and the body taken to the morgue.

Judy's mother arrived at my office with her second husband, Earl, and Judy's father, Arthur. The parents had divorced when Judy was a teenager but remained on friendly terms. Now, all three were sitting in my office's family room. They were grief stricken and in disbelief. Both the father and stepfather were demanding to see Judy's body.

The morgue was quiet that day. When I entered the family conference room, my heart went out to these grieving white-haired elders who had come so quickly to the hospital—Judy's mother with a walker and Earl with a cane. I decided at that moment that I would do whatever I could to help them. I explained that the morgue was at least a city block away through a maze of corridors and tunnels. Her mother decided to stay back in the office, but both men were undeterred. So, after half an hour of discussion and explanation about the circumstances and what they would see, these two old men and I started our walk to the morgue.

Earl was deliberate and slow in his steps, using a cane and hampered by a painful knee. Art, in contrast, walked quickly with a springy step, outdistancing Earl with each stride. I juggled to direct Art while waiting for Earl—not an easy task. As we arrived at the door to the morgue, the mood quickly changed as all energies focused on the task at hand.

We walked in and the door shut quietly behind us. We could see her body lying fully clothed on a cart and lightly covered with a clean white sheet. I walked up to her and gently pulled back the sheet.

While Art quickly strode up to Judy's side, Earl followed more slowly. Art bent down and brushed back her hair with his hand, kissed her cheek, and in a clear, soft voice said, "I love you babe, I always will. I know we'll meet again soon. 'Till then be good." Then he straightened up, brushed a tear from his eye, looked at me and matter-of-factly started asking about funeral arrangements, cremation, and the like. I could see that Earl had been hesitating, holding back, and now needed some time to be alone with Judy. Art, however, seemed oblivious to Earl's distress and continued to talk loudly, so I guided him and our conversation into the small morgue office a few feet away.

Art cheerfully told me that he was 80 and daily drove a bus for disabled senior citizens, how he recently joined a bowling league, and how much he enjoyed life. I had long ago come to expect almost any reaction from grieving family members, but Art seemed to be either in denial of the unfolding events or remarkably at ease—more confident than any parent I had ever encountered. After a few more moments, I commented to Art that he seemed to be handling a very difficult situation quite well.

He stopped talking, paused, and looked quickly and directly at me with his clear blue eyes. "Doc, I know the secret. . . ." I waited for him to continue. ". . . the secret about death. . . . I meant what I said to Judy; I know I'll see her again soon. I know it."

His blue eyes and snow white hair seemed even brighter for a moment. "You see, my mother told me about something that happened to her before I was born—it changed her life, and it has changed mine."

"Tell me," I encouraged.

"Well, when my mother, Mary, was in her 20's, she was diagnosed with a serious thyroid condition. She lived in Minneapolis and her doctor referred her to the University of Minnesota for her care. Dr. Wangenstein, Owen Wangenstein, became her doctor. You probably have heard of him."

"Oh yes," I said, "I know of him—he is a legend! He was the head of surgery at the University of Minnesota. . . ."

"My father, now a retired physician, was his student and had the utmost respect and admiration for Dr. Wangenstein," I added.

"Well," Art continued, "Dr. Wangenstein decided to operate on my mother's thyroid, to remove a part of it. Mother felt very good about the operation, but something happened during surgery, something went wrong. My mother said that all of a sudden she found herself looking down on her body from up near the ceiling lights. She saw the doctors working furiously on her but nothing seemed to help. She told me that she felt fine; she was happy and light. However, the operating room (OR) crew and Dr. Wangenstein in particular were shocked and dismayed, desperately trying everything they knew to save Mary's life. Finally, Dr. Wangenstein's assistant said, 'It looks like we lost her Owen. There is nothing more we can do.' The doctors and OR crew reluctantly stopped their frantic efforts and one by one left the operating room. Mother said she watched the whole thing, all the while feeling sorry for the doctors but not distressed for herself. She saw Dr. Wangenstein finally leave the room too, put his head in his hands, and heard him cry: 'No, no, no, I won't let this happen!' Then, all alone, he strode back into the OR where my mother's body lay draped with sterile sheets. He looked up at the ceiling and shouted, 'Mary! Mary come back! Stay with me here!!' And then he furiously began resuscitating her again.

"My mother remembered these events very clearly. (Mom called it her 'perfect recall.') She remembered being surrounded by swirling lights of many colors and somehow knowing that if she came back she would have a son. (That's me!)

"So she chose to slip back into her body and took a large breath. Dr. Wangenstein let out a whoop and shouted for the OR staff to return. The rest is history. He didn't leave my mother's side for the rest of the day."

"Did she ever tell Dr. Wangenstein what happened to her?" I asked.

"I don't know," Art responded, "but she and Dad got married later that year and I was born not too long after that. I have two younger sisters but no other brothers."

We both heard Earl blowing his nose, and I knew that he was getting ready to leave.

"Mom told me about that experience many times—it became our bedtime story. And one more thing Doc, my middle name is Owen. She named me that for Dr. Owen Wangenstein. She said she never wanted to forget her wonderful doctor who called her back, and she never wanted to forget the secret."

"There you go again, telling more stories!" Earl had shuffled up behind us. "Art loves to hear himself talk," he said apologetically to me.

Art was unperturbed. "Remember, Doc, now you know the secret too."

After I gently covered Judy's body with the sheet, we left the morgue and slowly made our way back to the office.

Both men thanked me for allowing them some time to say goodbye to their daughter.

It struck me how Art had such a spring in his step and a sparkle in his eye. His mother's wonderful experience, first whispered as a bedtime story, reinforced by a namesake, had changed a life.

# GREG'S GIFT

One hot Friday evening in June, 1995, authorities were called to investigate a motor vehicle fatality at an intersection in an industrial park on the northern edge of the metro area. A young man, just 22 years old and home from college for the summer, had gone to play softball with friends and stayed out late. While driving home on dark unfamiliar roads, for unknown reasons, he ignored a stop sign and collided with the side of a semi-boom truck. Another vehicle came upon the scene moments later, saw the tangled vehicles, and called 911. Sheriff's deputies and paramedics rushed to the area. The boom truck was loaded with ladders, scaffolding, electrical equipment, and construction gear. The mid-size car collided with the driver's side of the truck and was wedged beneath the truck bed. Debris was scattered over the roadway. The momentum of the crash caused the truck and car to skid over 20 feet from the site of the impact. The driver of the truck was unharmed, but badly shaken up. The driver of the car wasn't as lucky.

Paramedics who had rushed to the scene had climbed into the crumpled car as fire and rescue staff hastily jacked up the bed of the semi truck. The driver was collapsed in the seat, not moving. The crushed front end of the car had pushed the dashboard and steering column into the passenger compartment. They hastily cut away the driver's shirt, frantically searching for a pulse. EKG electrodes were slapped onto his chest—there was no pulse or respirations and no evidence of a heart beat. The "QUICK Combo" automatic defibrillator showed no cardiac activity, just a flat line. Blood was beginning to pool around his head. "Looks like head trauma," said the paramedic. No shock was indicated, and after checking with the ER doctor in the on-call emergency room, the young man was pronounced dead.

"Hard to believe that we lost him," said one paramedic, shaking his head dejectedly, "he was so young!" As he and his partner walked away slowly, hauling their gear with them, he called quietly to the sheriff's deputy, "Call for the coroner; he's gone!"

The death investigator on call responded to the scene quickly, donned his reflective vest, and walked through the yellow and red tape that cordoned off the area. Roger was a seasoned investigator who had worked for many years with the sheriff's office before retiring and coming to work for the coroner's office. The officer in charge recognized him immediately and began filling him in on the details of what had happened. "The state patrol's crash reconstruction specialist is on his way," he said. Roger nodded. "Have you identified him yet?" he asked the officer. "I've run the plates and they come back as a Gregory Bare. No warrants, no previous arrests—the kid looks clean if that's who we've got. I haven't touched the body yet." Roger began documenting the death scene as best he could in the dark, first with overall photos, then with close-up shots and a diagram. The path of the motor vehicle and the damage were recorded so they could be re-examined the following morning in the daylight. Next came the task of documenting the injuries to the body and making a positive identification. Roger pulled a wallet out of the back pant's pocket with a valid driver's license and photograph. The photo matched, and the vehicle was registered to the young man. A search of his body showed that his property consisted of a few personal effects; a checkbook, toothbrush and gold chain necklace were documented on a property sheet at the scene in the presence of law enforcement. Roger called for transport to the morgue—an autopsy was indicated to document the injuries and gather specimens for toxicology. The young man's family lived in northern Minnesota, and the state patrol would assist in notifying the family of his death.

The autopsy was performed the following morning by one of my colleagues.

The injuries were carefully photographed and documented, the clothing was removed and packaged, and the personal property was re-inventoried. Blood and body fluids were gathered, labeled, and sent for toxicology. The internal exam revealed the cause of death—massive head injuries  from the force of the impact with the truck.

My first conversation with Greg's mother, Mary, happened several weeks after his death. Mary, a nurse, had received a copy of the autopsy report and had questions. She had called my office and left a message. I pulled out Greg's file and reviewed it before dialing her number . . . severe head injuries, pronounced at the scene.

A woman answered the phone. "Hello, this is Dr. Amatuzio from the coroner's office. Is Mrs. or Mr. Bare at home?"

Mrs. Bare's voice sounded tearful, but gentle as she asked about the details of the report.

"I received the report in the mail, but I have a few questions about the injuries."

"Greg died from head injuries; they were quite severe," I answered.

"How bad were they, Doctor, I really have to know," she responded.

"When his vehicle collided with the side of the boom truck, he hit the windshield and the steering column. He wasn't wearing his seatbelt; his head struck the windshield causing massive head injury.

After a long pause, I heard her weeping. She finally asked, "Do you think there was any chance that Greg suffered?" That tender question is, perhaps, the one most frequently asked by family members who have lost a loved one suddenly or unexpectedly to injuries. The answer has to be based on fact, because when asked, it requires the highest degree of honesty.

"From the extent of his injuries, Mrs. Bare, I am almost certain that he would have lost consciousness immediately, and died shortly thereafter. The brain injuries were so severe that physically he could not have survived them." After a pause, I added, "I honestly cannot always answer that question, but in Greg's case, I can say that I'm almost certain he did not suffer. As you know, people were on the scene almost immediately. Greg never showed any signs of consciousness."

"Thank you for that. . . ." she said. This is just so hard; Greg and I were so close. He was such a whirlwind of energy and had so much to look forward to. . . ."

"I'm so sorry, Mrs. Bare. I can't even begin to imagine what you have been going through."

"Doctor," she said, "So many things have happened since Greg's accident. . . . I just don't know anymore. May I tell you something?"

"Yes" I said, uncertain of what would follow.

"When our two boys were young my husband and I hired a wonderful young woman, Sheila, to be the boys' babysitter. As things went on, the boys fell in love with her, and I guess that I did too. She referred to them fondly as her 'little boys' and would remind Greg of how she took care of him in his favorite blue sleeper pajamas. After the children were grown and off to college, she and I drifted apart. She moved to California; we would hear from her occasionally when she came home to visit her parents."

"I'm listening," I said.

She took a deep breath. "You are not going to believe what happened. Several weeks after Greg's accident, I was thinking about her and received a card in the mail from her that same day. After reading Sheila's card, I called her.

She told me that on the night that Greg died, she was awakened by a loud 'inaudible' voice that said, "Hey Sheila!" She sat up in bed. Greg was standing next to her. He seemed very distraught that he had caused his family and

friends such pain and sadness. She understood immediately
and comforted him as she had done so many times in the
past. Then he was gone. She said that she was somewhat
startled by his sudden appearance and departure, but that
she fell back asleep. Three nights later, however, she was
awakened again—this time by a gentle light and presence
filling her bedroom. And she saw Greg, my son, standing at
the foot of her bed. She was amazed; he seemed calm and
clear. He spoke to her and said, 'Please don't be startled.
Tell my mom I am fine; tell her I love her, and I am not
alone.' Sheila became aware of another presence with Greg,
his grandmother, my mother Verne. He stood there smiling
at her and then he was gone—the light in her room shimmered and faded. She called and subsequently found out
about Greg's accident. She felt compelled to write me.

"Your mother?" I asked.

"Verne, my own mother. She died from cancer 2 years
before Greg was born."

"You may think that I am crazy, Doctor, but that's not all.
Three nights after his death he also visited his girlfriend,
Trish, in much the same way. Trish awakened to see Greg

standing at the foot of her bed. She felt very calm. She asked Greg if he was okay and if he was alone. He told her that he was fine and certainly not alone. He said, 'There are so many people here.' "She was very comforted by his presence."

"What do you think this means, Doctor? So much has happened, and now this."

"Well, Mrs. Bare, the most important thing is what you feel about this."

She paused and I could hear her weeping once again. "At first I didn't know what to think but there is something that comforts me. I feel more peaceful. I feel they really did see Greg; that he is with my mother. I feel calmer now. This is all so strange, but somehow I know that he is still with us and that we'll see him again."

I thanked her, and marveled at it all.

# LETTING GO

Bill Hoogestraat is one of my heroes . . . and he is one of the scariest, kindest, gruffest, and wisest men I have ever met. He had been the captain in charge of the criminal investigative division of the Anoka County Sheriff's Office for 17 years and then became the chief deputy for 6 years. This man came to work for me as my office administrator, advisor, and friend. But Bill didn't just push paper in the office. He also frequently accompanied me to homicide scenes, conferences, and court testimonies.

When I began to relate some of the "unusual" stories I had been told, Bill's red bushy eyebrows would go up, he would shake his head and say, "You know, Janis, I really don't believe in that stuff."

One day after case review, we were sitting in my office and he said, "I have a story to tell you. . . ."

"What about?" I asked.

"Oh, you know, one of those stories about dreams and things."

"Tell me."

"Well, about 15 years ago or so, the sheriff's office was called to investigate a double shooting in the Heights—it was a murder-suicide. A 35-year-old man and his wife were arguing over their upcoming divorce. Neighbors overheard the quarrel. Later, her body was found in the kitchen with a gunshot wound to the head and his body was found in the garage, a .357 magnum handgun underneath him, with a gunshot wound to the chest. The medical examiner ruled their deaths murder-suicide after an extensive investigation by the sheriff's office and review of the autopsy findings.

"Now, the young man's father, Mr. Martin, just couldn't accept the ruling as murder-suicide. He could not believe that his son would do such a thing! He absolutely insisted that our conclusions were wrong and demanded that the case be re-opened. I called in the BCA (Bureau of Criminal Apprehension), who independently reviewed the facts and came to the same conclusion. Then the father insisted that the FBI (Federal Bureau of Investigation) review the findings, so after much discussion, I asked them to look at it as well. And as expected, they came to the same conclusion.

"Over all this time, Mr. Martin and I had many, many

discussions and talks. He was always a gentleman and respectful of my position, but he just couldn't accept the conclusion. In fact, after the FBI investigation, he'd stop in to see me about every 6 months or so. This became a ritual. One day, approximately 10 years after the deaths, he made an appointment to see me. My secretary pulled the file and made coffee. He arrived at the scheduled time, I greeted him, and he sat down in my office. This time when I opened up the file, he stopped me.

"'You know, Bill (by now we were on a first name basis), 'I don't want to go over the case again. I came to tell you that this will be my last visit . . . and how much I have appreciated your help, patience, and kindness over all these years.'

"'What changed,' I asked.

"The man sat there for a moment, hands folded, and thoughtfully proceeded: 'Well, you might not believe this, but I had a dream last week and my son came to visit me. He told me, "'Dad, you need to let this go. I made a mistake. I am so sorry that I have hurt you and Mom. But I'm okay now, and you have to let this go."' The man sat there for awhile after that and I was pretty astonished at what he had said. 'Bill, I know now that he did it, you were right all along.'

"We talked a little longer. I had really come to like him after all this time. And then we shook hands and he left. I remember telling this story to my lieutenant—we both didn't know what to make of it.

"A few weeks later, I was attending a conference in Mille Lacs County and the sheriff came up to me. 'Bill,' he said, 'George Martin died in his sleep a couple of weeks ago—I guess he won't be bothering you any more.'

"I was surprised." Bill said. "He really did 'let go.'"

# OH LORRAINE

One cold and snowy March day, late in the afternoon, I received a call from Anne, the on-duty hospital nursing supervisor, to report a death. "Doctor, I don't think this death is reportable to the coroner's office, but . . . I just wanted to check it out with you."

"Go ahead," I said.

"We have a 78-year-old man, Mr. Gardner, with severe congestive heart failure, who arrested and died this afternoon. He was admitted 3 days ago and was treated with digoxin, Lasix, Isordil, hydralazine, and oxygen at 5–6 liters per nasal cannula. He was also transfused with a couple units of packed cells."

"I agree with you Anne—that certainly sounds like a death due to documented natural disease."

"Well, Doctor, there's just one thing. He had a procedure this morning, a thoracentesis (a chest tap), to remove about a liter of fluid from the left chest. The doctor had no difficulty with the procedure but the patient didn't improve like we expected."

"I think I will look over his chart. The criteria for reportable cases include any deaths that are closely associated with a therapeutic or anesthetic procedure, but it sounds like he was pretty ill. Send the body to the morgue; I'll come down and review the chart this evening."

"Thank you, Doctor. Oh, one more thing, the patient's daughter is with him now. He is a widower, and she is concerned about the circumstances. She was with him when he arrested this afternoon."

"What's her name?"

"Rose."

"Tell Rose that I would like to talk with her."

"Okay, I'll put her phone number on the chart. Thank you," Anne said and hung up the phone.

My first step would be to review the chart, the second would be to talk with Mr. Gardner's physician.

As I walked down to the morgue, I thought about the number of deaths I had reviewed where, despite all the best that medicine had to offer, sometimes hearts and lungs failed and parents died. But the circumstances have to be explained and the family members reassured that someone is speaking for the deceased.

I quickly paged through Mr. Gardner's chart. He had a

history of two previous heart attacks, high blood pressure, and an elevated serum cholesterol—all the risk factors for heart failure—but something else caught my eye. Mr. Gardner had been married for 55 years and his beloved wife had died just 6 months earlier. He had evidently wrestled with the decision to spend the winter in Arizona since he and his spouse had gone there for many years. But then he decided to go to enjoy the company of the many friends he and his wife had there. In a letter from the referring physician in Sun City, I learned that Mr. Gardner's symptoms had been progressively worsening to the point that he was unable to walk more than a few steps before becoming short of breath. He decided to be hospitalized at home to be closer to his family.

Upon admission to the hospital, his heart was remarkably enlarged and dilated. It was clear that his heart was failing and his condition was serious. His physician had started all the appropriate measures and medications. On the morning of the third day, his doctor had apprised the family of the circumstances and recommended that the extra fluid that had accumulated in the chest cavity be removed to allow Mr. Gardner to breathe more easily. After the risks and benefits of the procedure were explained and agreed to by the family, the doctor proceeded to remove almost a liter from the left side of the chest.

I phoned Mr. Gardner's physician, Dr. Burns, a well-respected and gifted doctor, to ask how the procedure had gone and if death had been expected. Dr. Burns remarked, "Thank you for your call. My patient was a very sick man in the terminal stages of congestive heart failure. His cardiac output was dropping despite everything we could do. The chest tap, I felt, would improve the shortness of breath."

"Did you expect your patient to die this afternoon; I mean . . . are you surprised at the death?" I cautiously asked.

"Well to be perfectly honest with you, it was not expected today . . . but I am not surprised."

"Did the procedure go as planned?" I persisted.

"Well, I couldn't get any fluid at all on the first try, so I moved down one intercostal space before I had a fluid return. In my mind this wouldn't be uncommon. . . ."

We talked for a few more minutes.

"Thanks for your help and for your candor," I said. Sitting back down, I proceeded to once more pore over the chart.

Following the procedure, Mr. Gardner's blood pressure had dropped slightly throughout the day and his pulse had climbed from 80 to 130 beats per minute by mid-afternoon— a finding that can be associated with blood loss. The findings were subtle. In addition, he had evidently become less responsive. Initially, the nursing staff and family thought he was sleeping most of the afternoon, but his daughter became alarmed when she could not arouse him. The daughter called for help, and the responding nurse began CPR (cardiopulmonary resuscitation). It was a hunch, but I felt that I had to see with my own eyes what Mr. Gardner's chest cavity looked like.

I called his daughter, Rose Olson, and gently began asking her about her father and the events of the day. She was clearly grief stricken when she answered the phone that evening.

"Mrs. Olson? Mrs. Rose Olson?" I asked. "This is Dr. Amatuzio. I am a forensic pathologist and the county coroner. I wanted to tell you how sorry I am about the death of your father and explain why I am calling."

"Thank you, Doctor," she responded, her voice small and soft, "but before you begin you should know that I am a nurse and that I was with Dad all day today. I know his condition was very serious. I guess I knew he was . . . dying . . . but I am a little concerned about the chest tap. Dad had a lot of pain on that left side afterwards and his breathing got steadily worse instead of better. I am concerned that something went wrong."

Those were my thoughts as well. "That's the reason I'm calling. I know that your dad was very ill too. His congestive heart failure had remarkably worsened."

"A lot more since Mom died," Rose interrupted. "His heart had gotten steadily worse—he missed her so much."

"As I was saying, I feel we may want to take a look at your father's chest, particularly the left side to see if we can explain what happened."

"Our family would be pleased with that," she responded. "We knew the risks involved with the procedure and we accepted that, but I really must know what happened. I was so concerned this afternoon. I kept trying to arouse him, squeezing his hand." She began to cry. "I hope I didn't wait too long—I should have known. . . ."

"Mrs. Olson, Rose, now listen, please don't go down that path. Let's do the autopsy first, then we will talk."

"Okay," she agreed.

The next morning the autopsy was performed and the answers to our questions began to unfold. Mr. Gardner's left chest cavity contained almost a liter of blood. The needle initially used to pass through the chest wall had entered the chest cavity at a point where there was an adhesion, unbeknownst to the doctor, and had punctured the left lung. In other words, instead of passing into the space between the chest wall and lung where the fluid had accumulated due to heart failure, the needle had entered at a point where the lung was adhesed or "stuck" to the chest wall, puncturing the lung and causing it to start bleeding. The blood began to slowly accumulate in the left chest cavity, further compromising the function of the heart and lungs. His heart was badly diseased—the coronary arteries were almost totally plugged by cholesterol and plaque—and the heart appeared enlarged and dilated, certain evidence of the heart failure he had been experiencing.

I called the physician to make him aware of the findings. He was devastated. I assured him that he could not have known of the band of scar tissue creating the adhesion. Then, I called the decedent's daughter and informed her of the results. She listened quietly as I explained the puncture, the adhesion, and the extent of the heart disease.

"You know, Doctor," she said, "I am so grateful to the doctors and nurses for the care Dad received. And I appreciate knowing what happened. We realized that Dad's condition was quite serious and that he wouldn't be with us much longer. I am so glad I was there with him yesterday."

"I am sure he was comforted by your presence and your love," I said. "I am so sorry for your loss."

Rose paused, "There's just one more thing."

"Yes," I said.

"I have to ask one last thing."

"Go ahead."

"When I was sitting there at Dad's bedside yesterday afternoon, I got concerned because I couldn't arouse him even when I squeezed his shoulder and called his name. Just before I started to get up to call the nurse, my dad sat bolt upright in bed. His eyes were wide open looking straight ahead. He looked both astonished and delighted and he said in a loud clear voice, 'Oh, Lorraine!' Then he collapsed back in the bed . . . his eyes were still open. Even though I think he died right then and there, I ran for the nurse."

"Oh my," I replied. "Who is Lorraine?"

"Why, Lorraine is my mother. What do you think happened Doctor?"

"What do you think Rose?"

She hesitated and then in a soft, knowing voice stated, "Dad saw my mother, the love of his life, and she came to take him home."

"Thank you," I responded. "Thank you so much for sharing that beautiful moment with me."

"No, Doctor, thank you for listening and helping me understand what really happened."

Perhaps what really happened was that, even through the veil of her grief, Rose caught a glimpse of eternity. Perhaps she saw it—just for a moment through her father's eyes—and she recognized it as the truth about life.

What a grand parting gift these parents gave their daughter.

# BABY LOVE

My secretary came to the office door and knocked softly. "Your ten o'clock appointment is here—Ann Terry, the day-care woman. "

"Is she in the waiting room?" I asked.

"Yes and I gave her a cup of coffee."

"I'll be right there."

Two weeks earlier, on a Tuesday, Ann's life had changed forever when her best friend's baby boy, Jason, died at her day-care center. Ann was just devastated. Ann and Susie had been friends since childhood; they had grown up in the same neighborhood together and attended the same high school. When Ann married, Susie was her maid of honor, and several years later when Susie met her husband, Todd, Ann returned the favor.

Jason was born a year later, and Susie and Todd insisted that he go to Ann's day care when Susie went back to work.

On Tuesday, only his second day there, Susie had dropped him off in the morning. He was a smiley, happy, 3-and-a-half-month-old baby boy, who looked just like his mom. Ann had only one other child in the day care. The morning was calm; the baby was happy and played with all his toys. After his 11:00 feeding, she laid him down for a nap. When she went in to check on him an hour later, she was stunned to find that he was unresponsive and cold.

She immediately began CPR and called 911. Rescue personnel arrived quickly and rushed him to the local emergency room. Susie and Todd had been called at work and were rushing to the hospital. By the time they arrived, Jason had been pronounced dead.

Sudden deaths of infants are some of the most difficult deaths for anyone to handle. The parents and hospital and emergency staff are jolted from the expectation and promise of a young new life to the sudden shocking realization that it is over. The child, along with all the hopes and dreams, is gone. The loss can be overwhelming.

Susie and Todd had the chance to hold their first born and say goodbye at the hospital. They were put in a special, private room away from the emergency room and the hospital chaplain and others let them grieve in private.

The death investigator met with the parents and

explained the need for a postmortem examination. Then he gathered all the required information about Jason's medical history. The investigator also went out to the day care center and spoke with Ann, photographed the bed, and gathered information about the events of the morning. Jason had been placed on his back; he had been wearing a lightweight sleeper on a tightly pulled sheet that fit over the mattress. The crib and the day care facility were well kept. Ann, however, was understandably upset. The fact that Susie was her best friend added an enormous burden to her grief.

At the autopsy, Jason appeared to be a healthy, well-cared-for infant. His growth and development were excellent and there was no evidence of injury, infection, or congenital defect. Tests of his blood and body fluids were all normal. Jason's death was attributed to SIDS (Sudden Infant Death Syndrome). SIDS is also known as crib death, and most often affects infants two to four months of age, with a decline in incidence after this age. The diagnosis is made only when all other possible causes of death have been eliminated. Recently, there has been a slight decrease in SIDS since parents and childcare workers have been instructed to place infants on their backs rather than on their stomachs, and to keep cribs free of fluffy blankets or stuffed toys. This makes it easier for the infants to breathe and lessens the possibility that they could inadvertently suffocate.

I spoke to Jason's parents after the postmortem examination, told them that their baby looked beautifully cared for, and answered their questions. I informed them that I had received several messages from Ann. Susie told me that she had talked with her, but asked if I would speak with her as well, since Ann had many questions and felt responsible.

When I walked into the waiting room, I was struck with how young and frightened she looked.

"Ann, I'm Doctor Amatuzio. Thank you for coming in."

She stood up and shook my hand, glancing up only briefly. I could see that she had a wad of tissues in her other hand and that her eyes were red rimmed.

"Let's go into the conference room down the hall." She nodded and I led the way. We sat down.

"Your friend, Jason's mom, asked that I talk with you. . . ." With that she burst into tears, putting her hands up to her face. Her sobs filled the room.

"I feel like it's my fault. I let her down. Jason was so beautiful—I almost felt like he was in some ways my baby too!"

I proceeded to gently explain the features of SIDS as I handed her the box of tissues. "Ann, you must realize that this just wasn't in your hands—it appears you did everything correctly. There is no way you or anyone else could have predicted what happened, and there is no way you could have prevented it either."

Ann nodded and listened closely. We spoke for almost an hour and she seemed to become calmer. This was the first time anything like this had happened to her in the 3 years she'd been running the day care. It was clear that she was very deeply affected.

When I finished, she reached over and took my hand. "Thank you so much Doctor for taking the time to explain that to me. I have learned so much, from you and from Jason." She stood up to go and I stopped her.

"Ann, before you leave, would you mind telling me what you have learned from Jason's death?" I said.

"I'd be happy to tell you," she said as she sat back down, this time with an air of resolution and near confidence.

"I have learned more than I could ever have imagined from this. You see, I have a husband and two children of my own. I used to spend my time rushing from one thing to another. There never seemed to be enough time. I would fill my days to the max with all sorts of stuff, going here and there. I won't do that again. Jason's death was a wake-up call for me. I have taken the next 3 weeks off from work to get back to the important things. I'm taking time to write thank-you notes to everyone who has been so kind to me, I'm taking time to visit my dear aunt who lives in the nursing home, and I'm having lunch with my mother next week. I can't begin to tell you, Doctor, what has happened in me, but I even treasure the time I spend making dinner for my husband and kids. It all seems so precious to me right now."

Once again, I was grateful for the opportunity to hear a life-changing experience.

When she left, I just sat there in the conference room for a moment. The simple wisdom of living deliberately and thoughtfully had been so gracefully offered. "How had I forgotten something as important as this," I thought. Jason had given me a gift as well.

# GREAT-GRANDPA OLE

In the jurisdictions where I am appointed coroner, I train death investigators (who usually live in the county) to be my eyes and ears. They respond to the death scenes, possibly a motor vehicle accident on a snowy roadway, or a death at home, or even the hospital emergency room. Their duties include assisting in making a positive identification, documenting and logging all personal property, and notifying the next of kin. The scene investigation helps them make an initial determination of the probable manner of death and decide whether a postmortem examination is necessary.

The investigators are trained by me and my staff. They attend a 3-day course that includes lectures, observing an autopsy, and several practical or hands-on exercises. One of the evenings includes a dinner out together so we have a chance to relax and get to know one another.

One particular training session followed shortly after our office had handled a particularly difficult case—multiple fatalities in a single family, a tragedy for all. One of my new investigators, Mark, was a paramedic. He was bright and eager to learn and saw this training as an adjunct to his medical career. I was very happy to have him and enjoyed answering his questions.

At dinner that night, several of the new investigators had asked about the specifics of the case, but Mark sat back and listened. "I have a question for you," he said. "How do you handle the emotional stress of this job day after day. What keeps you going?"

The question caused everyone at the table to quiet down and look at me for an answer. I realized that, after all the cases they had seen over the past 2 days, they were asking for themselves as well.

"I feel that it's a privilege to care for these people at the time of their deaths. We have the opportunity to speak for those who have died. Our duty is most urgent for their families and loved ones. We help them understand 'what happened,' so they can grieve, reorder their lives, and go on living. That said, how do I handle it personally? Some of the things I have heard from their loved ones and some of my own experiences have caused me to believe that there is more to this life than meets the eye, and that gives me hope and helps me do this job."

"What kinds of things?" Mark persisted.

So I told my group of investigators the story of the young man whose mother told me about their babysitter in California, who had seen the young man in a dream on the night of his death. I told them that I could not prove anything from this, but that the story was comforting to me as well and helped me keep going and put my best effort forward each day.

Mark then said, "That's part of the reason I'm here too. You see, I had an experience myself and it has made me confident that I can handle this job."

"Tell us your story; we'd like to hear it!" said several of the investigators. And so Mark began:

"I grew up on a farm in a small southern Minnesota town near the Iowa border. My father's family lived on the farm too and his grandparents and great-grandparents were close by. We are Norwegians," he said as he smiled, "and we tend to live a long time!" We all laughed with him. "My great-grandparents had moved off the farm to a small house in town. When my father went back to school to train for a new job, we kids went to live with Great-grandpa Ole and Great-grandma Ida." He smiled as his eyes looked back over

the years, remembering. "Ole and Ida spoke Norwegian
better than they spoke English, and whenever Grandma Ida
would get mad at Ole, she would switch to Norwegian. We
knew that Ole was catchin' hell, but we didn't have a clue
what she was saying. I just loved my grandpa—he would
spend so much time with my twin brother and me. He took
us fishing on the river bank. I remember piling into his old
Ford. The dust would billow up through the floor boards as
we went sailing down those country gravel roads. We would
always stop and get Grandma Ida some fresh eggs from the
neighbors. He taught us how to whittle and talked to us
about the old country and his growing up. He would always
wave at everyone who passed by. Those were some of the
happiest days I can remember.

"Later on, we moved back with Mom and Dad on the
farm. It seemed to me that the 4 miles to Great-grandpa
Ole's house was an enormous distance, but soon I learned
to ride my bike over and my brother and I visited often.

"My twin brother and I had bunk beds. For some reason,
I always had the top bunk. One day when I was about 10 or
11, I remember waking up in the early morning hours because
I felt a weight on my legs, as if someone had just sat down on
the bed. I opened my eyes and saw Great-grandpa Ole sitting on the edge of the bed. It didn't dawn on me right then

that since I was on the top bunk it would have been hard for Ole to sit there like that. I just remember being delighted—so pleased that Ole had come over to visit. I remember that he just sat there and smiled at me and patted my leg. I said, 'What are you doing here Grandpa?' He just smiled back and said, 'Don't worry son. Everything will be all right.' I felt perfectly contented and assured. He continued to sit there, smiling. I quickly fell back to sleep.

"Several hours later, when I woke up, I was so happy because I knew that Great-grandpa Ole was visiting. I leaped out of bed and ran downstairs to find him. As I came bursting into the kitchen, I asked Mom and Dad where Grandpa was. They both turned around and stared at me.

"Grandpa Ole," I said, "Where is he?"

"What are you talking about?" My mother asked.

"Grandpa Ole woke me up when he sat on my bed last night."

My excitement turned to concern as I saw my mother and father suddenly turn pale. "Mark," my father said, "come over here to the table and sit down." My dad pulled a chair up next to me. "Son, I have some bad news to tell you. Your mother and I just had a phone call from the doctor. Grandpa Ole died in his sleep last night. Grandma Ida found him when she woke up this morning."

"I felt tears welling up in my eyes. 'No, no, no! That can't possibly be! He was here, he sat on my bed!' I remember that I started to cry. My mother walked up and put her arms around me. I buried my head in her arms.

"'Tell me about what happened last night,' she said calmly. I told her how I had been awakened by the pressure on my legs when he sat on the bed and how he smiled at me. I told her how very happy I felt because he was with me and how contented I was. 'Is there anything else?' she asked. 'Oh yes. He talked to me; he told me not to worry and that everything would be all right.'

"Mom's eyes filled up with tears. 'Mom,' I said, 'I saw him, he was fine, he was so natural.'

"'I believe you, Mark, and I believe that something very special happened to you last night. Most of all, I know how much Grandpa Ole loves you. Maybe we should remember the magic in his words, 'that everything is truly all right.'"

Mark sat back after he finished recounting the story. "You see Doc, you not only have me doing this job, you have Great-grandpa Ole."

# THE LOVING SPOONS

At 5:05 PM on a summer Tuesday, police and fire-rescue units were called to a home in a lovely residential area by the frantic call of a Mrs. Carson. "Help, help! I just got home from work and my husband is collapsed in the living room . . . I think he's dead!" she shouted to the 911 operator.

"What is your name?"

"Julie. Julie Carson."

"Is there anyone else in the home with you?"

"No, my kids are outside."

"Where is your husband? What is his name?"

"Randy. He's in the chair."

"The chair?"

"The chair in front of the TV set."

"Is he breathing?"

"No, I don't think so. He's all blue. I can hear sirens."

"Police are on their way. I'm going to talk you through CPR. . . ."

Officers arrived to find Mrs. Carson still on the phone with dispatchers, attempting to do CPR. Her husband's body lay on the floor next to his favorite plaid recliner where he had been seated. He was wearing blue jeans, a t-shirt, and a well-worn sweatshirt. The TV remote control was still clutched in his hand. Police made way for the paramedics who quickly applied the paddles to his chest. No shock was indicated—Mr. Carson was dead.

The officer on the scene called dispatch to notify the coroner's office and an investigator proceeded to the home. The paramedics left and one of the officers kept vigil with Julie until the investigator arrived.

I performed the autopsy the following day. In the majority of sudden, unexpected deaths in apparently healthy young adults, the cause of death is usually found in the heart although, on occasion, a ruptured blood vessel in the brain is the culprit.

An autopsy is an incredibly thorough examination of the external and internal aspects of the body after death. After the skin surfaces are carefully inspected, photographed, and described, the major organs of the chest and abdomen are

examined. Mr. Carson's heart and lungs appeared to be perfectly normal . . . that is, until I began to examine the left
ventricle of the heart. A large tumor, with finger-like
fronds, was growing out of the ventricular wall and floating
into the main chamber. I had never seen anything like it
before and was determined to discover if this was the cause
of his death.

With Mrs. Carson's permission, I asked for a consultation from a specialist to help interpret this unusual autopsy
finding. Mrs. Carson understood that the studies would
take a few weeks and the death certificate would be delayed.
(A death certificate is necessary for settling insurance
claims and other legal matters.)

As the weeks passed, Mrs. Carson called a few times
wondering if I had received any answers and, more importantly, wondering when I would formulate the death certificate. The "deferred" status was beginning to cause her some
financial strain.

One late Friday afternoon, I returned to the coroner's
office after a very busy day in the hospital laboratory. I was
looking forward to retreating quietly into the recesses of my
office to leisurely sort through the mail and charts on my
desk. My secretary, Sue, stood up when I walked in, a very
determined look in her eyes and a chart in hand. "Dr.

Amatuzio, if it's the last thing you do, you are going to call Mrs. Carson right now, or I'll lay down in front of the office door and block it!"

"Sue, Sue," I said, "it's 5:15, she won't possibly be home from work. Besides, I haven't yet received the consultant's report. . . ."

"Oh yes you have," she said waving an envelope at me. "It arrived this afternoon and Mrs. Carson has called me at least three times today looking for results. I promised her you would call and sign the death certificate today."

"Okay, okay," I said as I put both hands up in the air. I'll do it right now. I promise. You don't have to lay down in front of the door!" I joked with a smile. Sue was a substantial woman with a heart of gold. "Just let me review the chart first though."

The report was enlightening. The tumor was not cancerous, but instead a benign growth. However, one of the finger-like fronds had broken off, floated free, and entered one of the coronary arteries (the vessels which supply blood to the heart muscle). The tumor fragment was large enough to plug the vessel, acting just like a blood clot or fatty plaque, and stopped the flow of blood to a portion of the heart muscle causing a substantial myocardial infarct (heart attack). Now the whole story began to unfold. Mr. Carson had probably experienced an abnormal heart rhythm while seated in his recliner in front of the TV; the arrhythmia caused his death.

I formulated and signed the death certificate and handed it to Sue, who had generously offered to take it to the funeral home that evening. Mr. Carson had died of complications of a myocardial infarct due to a coronary artery tumor embolus from the primary tumor of the heart.

I heard Sue locking the office door as I was dialing Mrs. Carson's work number. Julie was an accountant. I am always reluctant to call when people are at work, but these circumstances were different and it was Friday, before a weekend. The receptionist answered the phone and quickly directed my call.

"Mrs. Carson, this is Dr. Amatuzio from the coroner's office calling to talk with you about the postmortem test results. . . ."

"What took you so long!!" she demanded. "I can't believe it took 3-and-a-half weeks! Don't you know that I have bills to pay and I have to have that death certificate?!"

"I am so sorry for the delay. These studies take time. I'm sure it has seemed like an eternity to you, but we had to have the correct answers," I gently offered.

"Well, what did they show? That's what you're finally calling me about, isn't it?!!"

She was angry, no doubt about it, but anger is often another manifestation of grief and loss, and I have come to expect it. "The report showed that the tumor in Randy's heart was benign, not cancerous. However, a piece of the tumor broke off and floated into the left coronary artery and plugged it. This blockage prevented blood from flowing to one part of the heart muscle and resulted in a heart attack."

"Well then, how did he die? Did he suffer?" she gasped.

"Mrs. Carson, Julie, when the heart muscle is damaged, it's prone to the onset of sudden abnormal heart rhythms that cause the heart to stop pumping. The brain quickly, suddenly loses consciousness and the body dies."

I could hear her crying now, low deep sobs. "Did he suffer?"

"Julie, remember how you found Randy—he was lying in his recliner, the TV was on, the remote was still in his right hand. Julie, the most likely thing that happened is that he experienced an arrhythmia and suddenly lost consciousness. There was no sign of a struggle. He simply and quietly slipped away, at home, in his favorite chair."

"With his favorite toy, the remote, in his right hand," she exclaimed, a faint smile in her voice. We both chuckled for a moment at her observation, glad to have some humor to ease the way. "Oh Doctor," she sighed, "I just don't understand all of this. It all seems so unreal. We buried him 3 weeks ago—it seems like a dream. I miss him so much!"

The tears welled up in my eyes, too. "I am so very sorry for you, I can't even begin to imagine how hard this is for you." I could hear her still crying. I glanced at the clock on my desk, 5:25 PM—the time had passed quickly. After a few moments I said, "Are you still there Julie?"

"Yes, I'm here . . . Doctor, . . . can I tell you something?"

"Of course," I said.

"I had something happen to me . . . after Randy died . . . I haven't dared tell anyone about it, but Randy came to visit me. . . ."

"Really! . . ." I said.

"Yes. Really, he did. . . ."

"Tell me about it," I said, feeling a shiver go through me.

"Well, as you probably know, Randy and I were married for 17 years and during all that wonderful time, we never spent a night apart. That first night after he died, I slept on the living room couch. We have two kids, a boy 12, and a girl 14. I wanted to hear them if they were up during the night . . . and I wanted to be near his recliner. I didn't sleep well at all. In fact, I didn't sleep at all. The second night I

gathered up my courage and laid down in our bed. I tossed
and turned all night. You know, I could smell him on the
sheets and all I could really do was weep."

As I listened to her, I thought of Elizabeth Kübler-Ross'
words from her book, *Living Until We Say Goodbye,* that, if we
dare to love, we must have the courage to grieve.

Julie continued, "I was exhausted, numbly making
funeral arrangements. The third night when I got back in
our bed, I started crying all over again. I'd reach for him
and he wasn't there. I think I finally fell asleep around
3:00 AM. At about 4:00 AM I was awakened by the sound
of footsteps in the hall. I sat up in bed, listening . . . thinking
it might be my son. I had closed our bedroom door so that
my sobbing wouldn't wake up the children. Doctor, the next
thing that happened was the most amazing thing that has
ever happened in my life. She paused and I waited. "It was
Randy, those were his footsteps. I saw him walk right through
our bedroom door. It was dark. I don't even have a night-
light, and I could see him clearly; he just glowed! He had a
wonderful smile on his face and walked right up to the bed. I
couldn't believe my eyes! I was shocked! We talked for a long
time. He told me what to do with our children and about
their future plans. We talked about the finances and the
property that I couldn't sell until I had that damn death

certificate!" (I now began to understand the urgency and the anger over the death certificate.) "But that was not all. I felt so calm, so reassured, so okay in his presence, for the first time in almost 4 days. I told him I didn't want him to leave and what he said then will last me a lifetime. I remember that while we were visiting, he sat on the bed next to me and had his hand on my shoulder. He wiped the tears from my eyes and told me that our love would be forever—that whenever I needed him to just think of him and he would come rushing to my side. He told me that I would feel his presence and love in my life many times and in many ways and that he would be there to help our children throughout their own lives. I can't even put it all in words, Doctor. There are no words to describe the comfort that I felt . . . but there is more.

"When we finished talking, I felt overwhelmed and wrapped up in his love. As I said, we had never slept apart and always slept wrapped together like spoons. As far fetched as this sounds, Randy then laid down in bed beside me and wrapped his arms around me." Her voice shaking a little, she added, "I felt the weight of his body and the warmth of it. I slept soundly and contentedly for the first time in 3 days."

"My, my, what a marvelous experience!" I said.

"Yes, when I awakened the next morning, I was overwhelmed and, most of all, comforted. I could feel that he was gone, but when I think of him now, I feel a warmth around my back and neck. I know that is his love."

She paused. "I still miss him so much though, this is so hard to get used to," she sighed. "I broke down and cried in front of the bananas at the grocery store last week. Randy just loved bananas. But by the time I got to the checkout line, I could feel the heat on my neck and I had to smile. I bought the bananas in spite of myself." We both laughed.

"I suppose I'd better get home to my kids. I have to gro-cery shop tonight," she laughed. "Thanks most of all for taking care of Randy and figuring out what happened and for letting me pour my heart out. I had to tell someone and I feel like you know him."

"You're welcome, you are so welcome," I said. "Sue, my secretary, dropped the signed death certificate off at the funeral home after work today; you should have it the first part of next week."

"Thank you, Doctor, you'll hear if I don't!! Good night."

I hung up the phone. The clock in my office now said 6:05 PM. I could hear the evening cleaning crew outside in the hallway, but I didn't move. I had been intrigued by the diagnosis on Randy's heart tissue, but I was amazed at what I had just heard. The intensity, the waves of grief, the tears, the anger . . . and then the visit. Nothing in my day, in my week, had compared to this. "What if," I thought, "what if it was true. . . ."

I packed up my briefcase, grabbed my keys and coat, and placed Randy's file back in the rolling bin for Sue. I thought for a moment on Randy's words, "Just your thought of me will send me rushing to your side." "I will remember that," I vowed.

# IT'S LIVING THAT COUNTS

An elderly woman had been brutally murdered in her home. The search for her assailant linked her death with yet another similar homicide. The death had been investigated by a number of law enforcement personnel in several different jurisdictions and by the coroner's office.

I remember the level of intensity of the search and the high emotions at the grand jury proceedings. A community is outraged when its perceived idea of security and safety is shattered by such a senseless act.

After the indictment, and faced with overwhelming evidence, the assailant pled guilty without a trial and was sentenced to life in prison without parole.

Following the events that brought the case to a conclusion, I was asked out to lunch by several key officials from the legal and law enforcement community, including the sheriff and the county attorney. The essence to solving and completing the case was the teamwork and cooperation. We were pleased with the work that had been done and the case conclusion.

The lunch conversation eventually drifted from the case to more leisurely topics like hunting, fishing, and vacation plans. At a lecture for detectives several years earlier, I had touched on the subject of immortality. The person who had arranged the lecture was at lunch with us and casually asked how my book was coming along. As I began to respond, it seemed as though all other conversation at the table stopped. This subject has a habit of causing people to do that and I found myself jolted from the comfortable feeling of coroner-forensic pathologist to treading on what I perceived to be the the shifty sands of "the fringe." One of the legal officials looked skeptical as I briefly explained that I was carefully writing down the stories I had heard from families and friends after the death of a loved one. I could feel their interest shielded with a healthy degree of "law-enforcement-type" skepticism.

I had decided to tactfully get off this subject, when the recently appointed sheriff, a competent, popular, and highly respected man, casually said, "Dying's not the big deal people make it out to be. I drowned once." I looked over at him, keenly aware of the implications of his statement. He didn't say "almost drowned," he said "drowned." I wondered what had really happened—the sheriff was not a man of many words.

"You grew up on Clearwater Lake, didn't you?" asked one of the other men. "Yes, my brothers and I spent just about every day of the summer swimming there. We used to dive off the lifeguard tower and race to touch the bottom of the lake and then turn around and race to the surface. As we got older that got too easy so we added a new twist. The old lifeguard tower had four legs, each of them constructed as a ladder. The rungs went all the way to the bottom.

"We decided to race by swimming in and out between the rungs all the way to the bottom, touching the lake floor, and then weaving our way back up, in and out through the rungs, until we got to the surface. The spaces between the rungs were wider at the bottom and seemed to get nar-rower near the top.

"That particular day, I was racing my brother to the top. I had only three or four more rungs to go when all of a sudden I got stuck! (There is a particular part of my anatomy that is well endowed in my family, he laughed, as he patted his hips.) And I mean stuck. I was really stuck! I was almost out of air and I started to struggle. I couldn't go forward and I couldn't back out. I was really wedged. I remember looking up and saw that my brother had made it. He was up on the surface just 2 to 3 feet above me, and he hadn't noticed that I wasn't on the surface yet. I remember that I started to panic." The sheriff's voice dwindled off and he seemed to be gazing inward across the span of years. "What happened next, Sheriff?" asked the county attorney.

"My brother went and told the lifeguard that I hadn't come up yet so they came down looking for me . . . pulled me right out of there, threw me into a lifeboat and started mouth to mouth. I 'came to' in the bottom of the boat— darn lucky I was. I remember that I had swallowed a lot of water. I was coughing and choking; it hurt to breathe. They took me in to shore and called my mother. My little brother was considered a hero—but I was grounded. We never tried that again!"

"We're all glad you made it to the surface, Sheriff, hips or no hips!" one of the men said.

I had the distinct feeling that there was more to the story—the sheriff was a very private man. I wondered if he would say more. "Sheriff, I asked quietly, 'How long were you out?'" "Oh, they tell me it was at least 10 minutes or so."

"Didn't you get taken to a hospital or ER?"

"Oh no, they just rowed me up on shore, made me lay

down, and called my mom. First she cried, then she grounded me for 2 weeks!"

"Do you remember anything from the time you realized that you were stuck underwater and couldn't get to the surface?"

The sheriff suddenly looked down, something about him changed. "Why yes, I do, but I don't usually talk about it."

"Go ahead, please tell us the rest of the story," said the county attorney. The sheriff paused and took a deep breath as if to clearly remember. "What happened is as clear as if it were yesterday," he said. I remember looking up at the surface of the water just out of reach. I began to panic, I was wedged in so tight and as I struggled harder I realized that I was out of breath. I remember thinking, 'I'm going to die, what a dumb way to die!'

"Then I took a large gulp of water and all of a sudden, the next thing I knew, I was up above my body looking down on it. There were beautiful colors everywhere. I felt sorry for my body, but it was strange; I wasn't worried about it. There was all sorts of activity going on frantically. The lifeguard and my brother and all sorts of people were there. I felt perfectly calm and found myself racing above the surface of the water, speeding along the surface really. It was fun. I could move by just thinking about it! I was surrounded by all these beautiful colors and I was heading toward shore when all of a sudden I was jolted back into my body! I was on the bottom of the boat, face down. The lifeguard was doing manual resuscitation and pumping on my chest. I remember the shock of being back and then I vomited.

"I seemed to slowly regain consciousness as they rowed me to the shore and carried me up on the beach. What I remember most was that when I looked around, everything seemed to be in black and white. It took several days till the color in my vision came back to normal.

"I wonder now if it was just that things were so stunningly vivid and bright when I found myself up above my body. It seemed that when I came back, everything looked a little dull."

We all sat there, still for a moment. I appreciated the sheriff's candor. He looked over at me with a smile, his blue eyes had a twinkle. "You know, Doc, I know that you are the coroner and see this stuff every day, and it bothers lots of folks. But I'm not afraid of death, not after what happened to me. Dying is easy, it's living that counts."

We all got up to leave, paid the bill, and headed our separate ways. I felt like the sheriff had given us all a gift that day . . . and I marveled at the coincidence, a wonderful synchronicity.

# PART IV

# SYNCHRONICITIES

There is more in this universe,
seen and unseen,
than the imagination can hold
or the heart can fathom

*Source unknown*

# MORE THAN
# A COINCIDENCE

Occasionally an event happens in one's life that seems too out of the ordinary to be merely a coincidence. At times these seem to happen almost on purpose—with a deliberateness that goes beyond understanding. One must pause and recognize something momentarily forgotten. Maybe there is no such thing as a coincidence.

How do we know when one occurs? We know. Our hearts are lightened and seem to skip a beat. For a moment we think differently and dare to hope there is more to life than previously imagined.

Some might call them signs, others might call them *synchronicities*.

# THE MONARCH

The cardiac rehabilitation center at the hospital where I currently practice is a vibrant refuge, filled with the young and old, patients and medical staff, using the treadmills, lifting weights, and sweating. I try to get there several times a week.

One day as I passed the treadmills, a coworker stopped me and told me that her father, age 70, had died unexpectedly. An aneurysm of the blood vessels at the base of the brain had ruptured, causing a massive stroke. He died suddenly in the hospital, 2 weeks later, of a pulmonary embolism (blood clot to the lungs) discovered at autopsy. I asked if there was anything I could do for her. Sadly she shook her head no; my heart went out to her.

One day a few months later, as I waved to her on my way to the NordicTrack, she stopped me and said, "Janis, do you remember when we talked about my Dad?" "Yes," I said.

"Well, there is something you could do for me, but I was a little hesitant to ask." "Go ahead," I said. "I meant it. What can I do?"

"Would you mind looking over my father's autopsy report? I have some questions."

"How about this afternoon?" I said. Although it was unusual, my afternoon was completely free that day. "I'll be there," she said.

She arrived and as I poured her a cup of coffee, I began to see her change. She became her father's daughter, struggling to understand what had really happened.

"I'm not here as a professional today," she said. "It's so incredibly hard to lose your dad. This feels like the worst thing that has ever happened to me. I miss him so much." She was fighting to keep back the tears.

I listened as she told me all the events surrounding her father's death, including the unusually persistent headache days before the aneurysm ruptured and his memory changes. As she spoke and I asked questions, a vivid picture of her father's hospital stay, subsequent discharge to a nursing home, and readmission to another hospital unfolded. She recounted the details with precision. She understood full well the risks of blood clots forming in persons who are inactive for long periods of time but wondered what more could have been done—or what had been missed.

"The doctors didn't really tell us about the severity and extent of the stroke—I guess I just didn't know what to expect."

"Well, sometimes the extent isn't fully known immediately, but let's look at the autopsy report; that should answer some of the questions," I said.

Her father's report showed evidence of a massive stroke on the left side involving all of the tissue in the distribution of a blood vessel known as the left anterior cerebral artery. The cause of the stroke became clear when we looked at the description of the blood vessels at the base of the brain, known as the Circle of Willis. Although the ruptured aneurysm had been repaired, the delicate balance of blood pressure and flow was disrupted. As a result, insufficient amounts of blood were delivered to the left anterior cerebral artery, causing damage—a stroke.

She sat quietly for awhile when we finished.

"Thank you for explaining that to me, thank you for taking the time."

"I'm glad I could help. Autopsy reports can be difficult to understand, even more so when it's your own father."

"I have something else to tell you, something that happened to Mom after Dad died."

"Go ahead," I said.

"Mom and Dad live on a lake and have a beautiful garden. Dad loved to tend the garden and he loved butterflies. One of my sisters stayed with Mom for the first couple of weeks after Dad died. It was such a difficult time for us, but for Mom especially. She would sometimes stand out in the backyard in the garden and wonder where he had gone and where he was now. That summer a mother duck had started bringing her ducklings up on shore into Mom's yard. Mom enjoyed their company.

"One day a few weeks later, my sister brought her 5-year-old daughter, Mom's granddaughter, over to visit and watch the ducks. While Samantha was playing, and my sister was visiting with Mom, Samantha came running up to her grandmother and said, "Grams, do you think Papa could be a butterfly now?" Mom laughed and said, "No dear, Papa is in heaven now. I don't think he is a butterfly."

"That evening, Mom sat down in the living room to watch TV after everyone had gone home. It was early August, almost 9:00 PM; the sunset had been full and vibrant in the western sky. The garden was in full bloom and its fragrance filled the air. Mom had latched the screen door and was sitting in her reclining chair, her hands cupped in her lap. Quite unexpectedly, she noticed a monarch butterfly fly gracefully across the living room in front of the TV and alight softly in the palm of her hand. She was amazed it landed softly in her hand. She had never seen a butterfly in her house before. They both sat there, she and the graceful monarch butterfly. Mom didn't move; the butterfly slowly fanned its wings. It was the largest butterfly she had ever seen, but more importantly, she remembered with a shiver, Monarchs were her husband's favorite.

"In that moment, she became aware of a gentle peacefulness that surrounded her like the warmth of the sunshine at first light. She knew in her heart that, without a doubt, somehow her husband was fine, that all was well. As she thinks back on it now, she believes her heart began to heal that night.

"After a little while, she gently cupped her other hand around the butterfly, carried it outside to the patio, and set it on a flowering plant. Even though it rained later that night, the large monarch was still there in the morning and stayed till midday. Just long enough to reassure Mom. It left as it had arrived.

"Mom still greatly misses Dad, but now she has a picture of a monarch butterfly next to him on her desk. I know it reminds her of his love."

# PINK PEONIES

I was thrilled when I was appointed Coroner for Anoka County! It was 1993. Although I had 10 years' experience as an assistant coroner in another regional system, this was the first time I headed a department.

Because I was busy with the demands of the surgical pathology department at the hospital, and directing the clinical laboratories at two other hospitals, it was clear that I needed to find a secretary. It was important to choose just the right person, one I could depend on and trust.

As it turned out, I didn't find Sue—she found me. She had seen the ad and called for an interview that same afternoon. I had just finished reading out my surgical slides when my office door frame was filled by a large woman with bright blond hair (pulled back in a comb) and long pink fingernails. With an assertive air, she walked into my office, sat down, and said, "I think I am the one for the job. But, first, I have to ask you some questions!!"

In the ensuing hour, I had the distinct impression that I was the one being interviewed. She had a hearty laugh, a no nonsense manner, and a firm idea of what she wanted. Most of all, I sensed that she had a heart of gold. I hired her 2 days later and we began an odyssey that would last some 5 years. Little did I know that it would be Sue's last job on earth.

Sue had worked as an executive assistant before coming to the hospital to work as a phlebotomy technician. She had never married and lived with her mother, Bea, in northeast Minneapolis. She liked to tend her garden, shop at garage sales, and spend time with her sister and friends. Sue was always remembering a birthday or anniversary, sending flowers, or graciously offering a guest a cup of coffee. She took care of everybody.

We set up an office in a tiny two-room suite in the basement of the doctors' office building. We gathered used furniture from the county government center and the hospital. Pretty soon we had an abundance of used chairs, desks, and file cabinets. Not surprisingly, none of them matched. Because family members would sometimes come to the office to pick up property or to meet with one of the pathologists, Sue suggested that we reupholster several of the chairs so that the office would look more professional and inviting. I wholeheartedly agreed.

Sue loved the color pink . . . not exactly the shade you might expect to see in a coroner's office lobby. She picked out a soft shade of rose for the chairs and couch and accented everything else in maroon. She chose a picture of pink and white peonies and had it framed for the wall. It hangs in our office waiting room still. One day, she proudly displayed some matching pink silk flowers that she had found, arranging them in a maroon plastic vase to accent the little table next to the couch. Her touch made the office seem inviting and comfortable.

In the spring of 1996, 3 years after we had begun working together, Sue began feeling ill and seemed to fatigue easily. She had slipped and fallen on the front steps of her home that March and had fractured her ankle. She was in a cast and on crutches for several weeks and had obtained a temporary "handicap" sticker for the office parking lot. As May passed into June, Sue seemed reluctant to give up her crutches. She was still experiencing pain, this time in her hip and knee. She had consulted her doctor, her ankle had healed, and there was no explanation for the other aches, pains, and weakness.

Sue kept most of this to herself. The summer passed and she began using a cane. I urged her to see another doctor and get a complete physical. One day in August, she asked me what the blood test "alkaline phosphatase" was for. I told her that it was an enzyme found in the liver and in bone. An elevation of this enzyme in the blood could signify abnormality in either. She then confided that her blood tests revealed an elevated alkaline phosphatase level as well as an elevated erythrocyte sedimentation rate—a test that can show extra proteins from acute or chronic inflammation or other conditions.

Because of her bone pain and abnormal lab tests, her physician had ordered a bone scan. Sue had scheduled it late in the day so she would not have to miss work. She cautiously asked if I was planning to stay late that day and then shyly told me that she would appreciate it if I could hear preliminary results from the radiologist. There was a nagging feeling in the back of my mind that something was wrong, seriously wrong. I knew that I was walking the fine line between physician, employer, and friend.

There are always some moments in one's life that stand out in memory forever with vivid clarity. I think those moments mark a change; you realize that things will never be the same again.

That evening I had one of those moments. I had wandered over to the radiology department after leaving the cafeteria. One of the techs who I knew—and who knew Sue—was at the front desk. I asked how Sue's scan was going and she told me the initial X rays were just being developed. I was handed several films in a folder.

When I placed the films on the X-ray view box, I was overwhelmed by what I saw. There were more areas of bone that "lit-up" than I could count. There was only one thing that could give this pattern: widespread malignancy, metastatic cancer. I remember the tears filling my eyes as I saw all the spots throughout her ribs, spine, hips, arms, legs, and skull. Her bones were riddled.

Sue had breast cancer. She had noticed a lump on her left breast several weeks earlier but hadn't given it much thought. The tumor had spread to her bones and lymph nodes. Her treatment was aimed only at controlling the cancer—there was no hope for a cure. She stopped working and began an intensive series of radiation therapy sessions. The day after she cleaned out her desk, I found a lovely card. The front was covered with lovely pink peonies, the inside was a thank-you for my concern and care.

Sue handled the next 3 years with courage, intermixed with excruciating pain and many tears. The disease was unyielding and relentless. As her body deteriorated, she struggled to stay involved, and her friends circled around her in a web of love.

In December 1998, Sue was determined to have one last Christmas with her family. I think it was primarily her sheer force of will that kept her alive. She was admitted to the hospital the day after Christmas and died there on January 6, 1999, in the presence of her mother, sisters, and close friends.

My busy growing practice pulled me back into full swing. Two secretaries now filled Sue's position. Our original office space had become cramped and was filled to overflowing with files and desks. That next fall we decided to remodel and expand our work space. This time the plans included a family room—to be comfortable and comforting for grieving families. A white couch, chairs, and a small water fountain filled the small space, making it private and intimate. The picture of the pink and white peonies, Sue's favorite, hangs in the room over the couch.

In the course of our remodeling, the pink silk flowers and maroon vase had been discarded. They had become dusty and, with our growing need for space, had been placed on a shelf, then in a closet, and eventually in a dumpster.

The remodeling project finished 2 days before

Christmas—just in time for our open house. The new jewel green carpet, ivory walls, and jade-colored desktops in the reception area just glowed. Well wishers, poinsettias, and an enormous bouquet of roses arrived from the building manager. All who came to visit that day were pleased with the changes. But the room that everybody loved best was the family waiting room. With its low light, people pushed their chairs in and sat there, absorbed in conversation and strangely reluctant to leave.

My guests weren't the only ones who treasured that room. The cleaning staff in my building is directed by a wonderful, gracious woman named Tammy. Her laughter and smile always precede her down the corridors. Unlike others, Tammy was never daunted by caring for the "Coroner's" office. Tammy immediately made the family room her own and made no secret of the fact she would often spend a few minutes there peacefully collecting her thoughts.

I was working late one January evening. The cleaning crew usually work until 8:30 or 9:00 PM, but after that the building is empty and the halls are dark. Tammy made a habit of checking to see that all the office lights were turned off.

"I'll be back to check on you before we all head home,"

she said, "and I have a little present for you—for the waiting room." "Okay," I answered as she left. I would get more paperwork accomplished in the solitude of the evening hours than I could during the busy day. The time passed quickly and I again heard Tammy at the front door. It was about 8:30. The staff had started to turn off the hallway lights. "Janis, I'm back . . . come see the little surprise I have for you." I walked out of my office, glad to be finishing the day. Tammy was standing in the doorway to the waiting room, a gleam in her eye. With a big smile she gestured to the little end table. There sat the battered maroon vase filled with Sue's slightly dusty, tattered pink peonies.

"Where did you find these?" I asked in amazement. "Why Janis, they were in the dumpster last fall. I knew they were Sue's and I just couldn't let them go."

"Tammy," I said suddenly, glancing at the calender, "Do you know what day this is?"

"Why yes, Janis, its Tuesday, January 6th."

"Tammy, I just realized that Sue died 1 year ago today!" I said.

We both just stood there and looked at one another and then at the flowers. Then laughter and tears swept over us as we remembered Susie.

The following day I relayed the events to my friend and

office manager, Kay Cooper. She looked at the somewhat bedraggled bouquet with me. Kay had the errant silk pink peonies cleaned and placed in a lovely silk flower arrangement that sits on our front desk to this day. As for the maroon plastic vase, it has vanished.

# A FATHER'S GIFT—
## "4:20 PM"

After a lecture presented to the Hennepin County
Medical Society, one of my colleagues, an emergency room
physician, came up to me to tell me about her father and
the synchronous events that occurred around his death.

"My father was diagnosed with cancer and, after numerous
chemotherapy and radiation treatments, he went home to
spend the time with my mother before he died. I knew his
condition was worsening but had committed to attending a
medical conference in Miami. He urged me to go and told
me he would be fine. I reluctantly agreed and kissed him
goodbye.

"My travel arrangements included transferring planes in Atlanta. I had just found my seat on the plane, buckled up, and was sitting there when something extraordinary happened to me. I was overcome by the most incredible feeling of joy—like a wave of ecstasy—like time was suspended. It took my breath away. I was filled with peace and became extraordinarily calm. It was amazing! I glanced at my wrist-watch: it was 4:20 PM. For the rest of the flight, I didn't even read the book that I brought along. I was so moved by what had happened to me.

"When I reached Miami, I called my mother. She told me that my beloved father had died peacefully while she sat at his side . . . at 4:20 in the afternoon!

"Later, as the family gathered to honor his life and to grieve, my sister, who was working in Seattle at the time, told me about something that happened on the afternoon Dad died. She was on an elevator and when all the others got off, the doors closed and the elevator began to move. It suddenly stopped for a moment and all of the floor lights began to blink wildly. Then the elevator delivered her safely to her floor. When she got off the elevator, she glanced at her wristwatch: the time was 4:20 PM."

"Barb, what did you make of all that?" I asked.

"That was Dad's way of saying 'Goodbye.' He truly let me know that he was 'just fine.'"

# SYNCHRONICITY AND MRS. BROWN

**M**rs. Brown is David's mother, a proper, petite, kind, and gentle Irish woman with pretty blue eyes and a lilting laugh. I met her only once, at David's wedding, but felt as though I knew her, because her son, my good friend, spoke of her so often. She was wearing a pretty rose-colored suede suit, which made her cheeks glow pink. Her snow white hair was curled gently around her face.

David and Janet were married outdoors, at home, on a beautiful late September Saturday when the sky was a brilliant blue, the hillsides were sunkist with gold and red, and the breeze playfully tossed the prairie grasses. Friends mingled and good will, champagne, food, and conversations were abundant.

The day was special in many ways. I was aware that Margaret Brown had been diagnosed with widespread cancer several months earlier. When we sat to visit for awhile, she beamed and laughed and looked just beautiful. I remember thinking how brightly her light was shining and about the treasure of each moment.

Margaret's health slowly faded. David never missed an opportunity to be with her, often taking her out to lunch or driving her out along the river bluffs and rolling grassland that she loved. In the days and weeks before her death, she was constantly surrounded by her family and close friends. She gave many special gifts to her children and grandchildren and took time to share her wisdom and counsel with each one. She left this world gently, at home, on a February afternoon, with her family surrounding her.

David called me early that evening to tell me that his mother had died. I listened as he recounted the day's events in a weary but steady voice.

"You know, Janis," he said, "after she passed, I stepped outside. It was 2:20 in the afternoon. I needed a few moments to myself. I let the tears come and felt the icy wind sting my cheeks. Nothing ever prepares you for something like this. I looked up and wondered where she was now and told her again how much I loved her. The next thing that happened amazed me," he said. "An owl, a nocturnal bird, suddenly swooped down and flew right in front of my face. It came so close that I stepped back and caught my breath. I wondered for a moment if Mom was letting me know that she was just fine. I felt better somehow after that happened, and Janis, I thought about some of the synchronicities you have told me."

As I listened, I remembered the significance of the owl in Native American culture. In many traditions, the owl is a symbol of transition, of a passing from one life to another. Many times, an owl is seen or heard just before the death of a tribesman. This belief was beautifully explained in the book by Margaret Craven, *I Heard the Owl Call My Name.*

I told David how sorry I was for him and his family. I too wondered at the synchronicity of the owl, and felt in my heart that Margaret had comforted her cherished son in her own gentle way.

Later that evening, when I was sitting at home on the porch with my dogs, I thought again about Mrs. Brown and David and the owl. I phoned my parents in Arizona to talk and, I think, to comfort myself. They were vacationing near Sun City, in 80-degree temps and bright sunny days. I was happy for them. My husband was working, so the house was quiet and the evening drew to a close. I felt the loss, too, remembering Mrs.Brown's bright blue eyes and her pink suede suite. I whispered a prayer for her and her family.

That night the sky was clear and star studded when I let the dogs out in the backyard so I slipped on a jacket and went out with them. It was extraordinarily cold and quiet. My loyal rottweiler, Magic, was standing by my side when all of a sudden I heard a rhythmic "whoosh whoosh whoosh" of wings. My eyes quickly scanned the night sky . . . but I saw nothing. The sound grew louder and my heart began to beat faster in my chest. Still nothing in the sky except the stars and the moon!

As I think back on it now, I laugh at myself because I became so alarmed. My palms began to sweat. I couldn't see a winged bird anywhere and I thought that just maybe I was hearing angels' wings! I quickly looked down at my dog and much to my relief he was hearing something too . . . at least his ears were up and his brow was furrowed.

Then I saw them, in the brilliant night sky, against the moon. A vee of canadian geese, flying low. I let out a sigh, still slightly rattled by the evening's events and more than a little amused at myself. But what happened next, I can't explain with any logic at all. As Magic and I watched, the geese flew overhead, the rhythmic sound of their wings grew fainter and then louder. The geese slowly circled back over me, not once but twice. And each time they flew over my head they formed a perfect "J" in formation.

I was stunned. The first time it happened I felt it had to be a coincidence, but my doubt turned to amazement when they flew back and formed the "J" again. I was reminded that there is no such thing as coincidence and I was filled with a knowing . . . that all was well with Mrs. Brown.

"Thank you Mrs. Brown," I whispered. "Thank you, bless you, and Godspeed."

The simple elegance and power of her message will not be forgotten. I realized only later the beauty of the symbol of the geese. When the season is right, the geese migrate to a new place and begin their lives all over again. Mrs. Brown just pointed the way.

# PART V

# IN SIGHT

Won't you let me know
that life is eternal
and love is immortal
and death is only a horizon...
And a horizon is nothing
Save the limit of our sight.

*Rossiter Worthington Raymond*

# IN SIGHT

At times in life we observe, and at times we really see. This seems to be the beginning of understanding—the foundation for wisdom.

When Proust wrote, "The path to wisdom is not in seeing new vistas, but in having new eyes," he may have been alluding that understanding has to come from within. As we live and love, life's real messages and meanings come from looking within, from reflecting, and observing what speaks to our soul. In the process we develop 'insight'.

The following experiences could be viewed as simply interesting stories . . . or they could be read with new eyes. It may be that our loved ones are not really gone. If we look with new eyes, we may see that they have been with us all along—in all the difficult and trying times of our lives—surrounding us with their love and blessings.

Maybe they are truly

in sight.

# A MOMENT OF GRACE

This story was shared with me by Pat, a physical therapist who works in cardiac rehabilitation. She gently supervises the exercise programs of her patients and encourages those of us who use the NordicTrack at lunch time.

❧

"In June 1988, my dear mother, Eileen, learned why she was having terrible abdominal pain and couldn't eat normally. Doctors at Mayo Clinic discovered pancreatic cancer, and their prognosis gave her 4 to 6 months to live. She was advised that there was a 40 percent chance chemotherapy might decrease the tumor by half. With her practical and faith-filled approach to life, she declined the treatment. My mother died October 5, 1988, at her home with her family around her.

"Ten years later in December of 1998, my son's mother-in-law, Dorine, began feeling pain in her abdomen and also had difficulty eating. Her symptoms reminded me of my mother's experience. My fears were realized when, after nearly 6 weeks of testing, Dorine was diagnosed with pancreatic cancer. The doctors thought she had about 1 year to live.

"Dorine started on a regimen of chemotherapy, which made her weak and nauseated. The treatment went on for several weeks. During this time, I visited her and her husband, Al, when I could. One day, I told them about my mother's illness and her decision not to undergo any chemotherapy because her doctors had said it wouldn't cure her (though it might give her a few more months to live). I thought the doctors' prediction of 1 year of life for Dorine might be overly optimistic and I hoped Al wasn't counting on that much time for his wife.

"Dorine spent her time at home on heavy pain medication. However, her pain became so terrible that she was taken to Abbott Northwestern Hospital. She and Al were accompanied to the emergency room by their children, Tim and Colleen. They had forgotten Dorine's medications, so Tim and Al returned to get them. Colleen remained with her mother, comforting her as she lay on a cart in the emergency room. Colleen also was awaiting her husband, Ted, who is my son.

"Dorine drifted in and out of sleep. At one point, she awoke and calmly looked around. She asked Colleen, 'Is that Pat's mom over there?'

"Colleen was surprised by the question, but responded, 'I don't know. Did she introduce herself?'

"Dorine answered, 'Yes, she did,' and fell asleep, peacefully.

"Dorine was admitted to the hospital. A nurse told the family that their wife and mother was dying. They said their goodbyes and expressed their love. Two days later, May 5, 1999, Dorine died.

"The incident in the emergency room has been a comfort for Dorine's family and for me. Two families were blessed by Eileen's presence that day. I think it was a miracle, a moment of grace. The two women had not known each other in life, but their connections were a common mortal illness and my son, Ted, a son-in-law to one and grandson to the other. I believe my mother was welcoming Dorine to heaven. They are now together for eternity."

# THE BOOK OF LIFE

The hospital basement has a life of its own—the hallways twist and turn like a maze. The security office, credit union, and laundry are nestled together in one area. The elevators separate the rest of the hallways from the maintenance department and, lastly, the morgue.

One day Dr. John Alexander, a smart deephearted internist, pursued me down the hallway. "I heard your lecture last week, and I have a story for you," he announced.

"I'd love to hear it, but I just don't have time right now," I blurted out, "Unfortunately, I have four waiting for me in the morgue."

"You'll want to hear this one, Janis, and besides, I tracked you all the way from the tunnel to tell you," he said with a note of urgency. The hallway bustled with people and large carts. John and I found ourselves at the open door of the hospital laundry, the only quiet place one could find.

We walked in and stood there amid the calm stacks of clean sheets and fresh towels as he shared this deeply moving experience.

"Janis, when I started in practice here, you know the times were different. The hospital staff was small, and we all knew each other quite well. There was a real spirit of camaraderie."

"Yes," I nodded.

"Do you remember Dr. Tom Rice?"

"The name is familiar, John, but I don't recall him specifically."

"He was a hard-charging family practice doc and one of the original group on the staff when I came here. He had a wonderful personality and a great sense of humor and was dearly loved by his patients and colleagues. He developed carcinoma in his early 40's and was determined to beat it. He had already gone through surgery and the first course of chemotherapy when he asked me to be his physician. He didn't let the cancer slow him down. He still kept a busy practice and raised a young family.

"The hospital staff, both doctors and nurses, intensely admired him and were fiercely protective. He had forged many strong friendships among them. Unfortunately, 3 years after the initial surgery, the tumor recurred in his lungs, showing up first in a routine chest X ray. Tom chose to try a new, aggressive form of chemotherapy, which then was only offered at the University of Minnesota Hospital.

"He decided to be admitted there for several days because of the possible side effects. I went to visit him one evening after I finished my rounds here. He was in a small private room not far from the nurses' station. When I walked in, I could hear that he was in trouble. His breathing was labored and heavy, his breath sounds raspy and irregular. I reached for my stethoscope and quickly listened to his chest. The breath sounds were muffled and faint. Tom's eyes opened slightly, but he didn't seem to recognize me. He was in pulmonary edema (a condition where the lungs fill with fluid, compromising their ability to exchange carbon dioxide for oxygen), a common side effect of that type of chemotherapy. I ran down the hall and called for a nurse.

"'Dr. Rice is in pulmonary edema. I need you in there now and I need one of the house staff here stat!'"

"'They're all at a Code Blue in the emergency room,'" she said, "'And who are you?'"

"'I'm Dr. Alexander. Dr. Rice is my patient and he needs Lasix and morphine IV push now and nasal oxygen or we will have another Code Blue right here. Now are you going to get it or should I?'"

"She looked at me, a bit startled, and rushed into the room with me. Her uncertainty lasted only seconds and she looked at me again."

"'I'm not on this hospital staff but I'll take responsibility. He needs 40 mg of Lasix and 5 mg of morphine IV push now.'"

"'I'll get it,'" she said, running down the hall to the nurses' station."

"Later that evening as I sat by Tom's bed, his breathing finally back to normal, he turned his head and opened his eyes. "'John, what are you doing here?'" he asked.

"'I just stopped by to visit you, Tom, and helped a little with adjusting your meds.'"

"'You know, John, I was someplace else just now.'"

"'Really? Where?'" I asked.

"'I found myself trying to cross this lake, and the water kept getting deeper and deeper. I had trouble keeping my head above water—I kept going under. But you know John I had to keep going because I could see my house on the shore; it was all lit up and my family was there. It's hard to explain, but I had to keep breathing for them. Every time I took a breath it was as though the house filled with life. I guess I kept my head above the water,'" he said.

"'Yes, you did,'" I said, as I marveled at his intuitive metaphor.

"The chemotherapy stopped the growth of the tumors in his body for a while. Some even disappeared. Perhaps on some level, Tom knew this. He returned to work—this time at almost a feverish pace. Those who didn't know him marveled. Those who did know him understood that his frantic pace in some way may have been Tom's attempt to outrace the tumor and embrace his life.

"Friends and physicians grew increasingly concerned as Tom became thin and gaunt, but there was no stopping him. One late afternoon, I saw him striding down the hallway. He looked tired. As his eye caught mine, I noticed for the first time a hint of jaundice in the whites of his eyes. "'Tom,'" I said, "'How are you doing?'

"He looked at me wearily. 'Not as good as I thought,' he said.

"'Let's go down to the lab to draw some blood work on you.'

"'What do you suspect,' he asked, looking at me sharply.

"'I think we better do some liver function tests. You look a little jaundiced.'

"The tests were abnormal and the liver scan that evening told the rest of the story. The tumor had recurred again, this time with a vengeance.

"Tom was admitted to the ICU (intensive care unit) that very evening and for the first time in all the years I had cared for him, it seemed as though the fight had gone out of him. He looked both tired and fragile in the hospital bed. And although I knew he didn't want to be there, he was content to rest a while. I stayed until midnight, stabilizing his blood work and organizing his care. He was sleeping when I left."

"I didn't rest well that night and got up early to head back to the hospital. I walked into the ICU at 5:30 AM. The nurses were surprised to see me and assured me Dr. Rice had slept most of the night.

"I went to his bedside and stood quietly for a moment. Tom must have heard me because he slowly opened his eyes, which appeared more deeply jaundiced. 'John,' he said.

"'How are you feeling, Tom?'

"'Fine, John, better than fine,' he said to my surprise.

"'John,' he said with a new look in his eye, 'I read an amazing book last night, cover to cover.'

"'Really,' I replied, 'and what book was that, Tom?'

"'The Book of Life, John and,' he paused, 'my name was in it.'

"'How did it end, Tom?'

"'Fine, just fine. Everyone was okay,' he responded.

"In that instant something tugged at my heart—I was immediately aware of the deep comfort in those words. I reached over and gently grasped his hand. Making an intuitive leap, I asked, 'Tom, do you want to move to a private room today?'

"'Yes, 'he said, 'I'm ready to go home.'

"I looked deeply into his eyes. 'I'll call your wife and tell her.'

"I moved Tom to a private room, which filled that morning with his close family. He told them of his dream, and died quietly that morning in their loving presence at 11:00 AM."

Dr. Alexander looked me in the eye as I stood there in the hospital laundry, amazed and deeply moved at the breathtaking beauty of the story. "That's not all, Janis," he said. "I really took some heat from the medical staff for the decision to stop intensive therapy. Tom had been such a fighter.

I think some of them thought I had let him down. I really struggled and think I second guessed my decision too.

"One day several months later, I was in the hospital elevator after lunch, when one of the nurses I faintly recognized tapped me on the shoulder. 'Could I talk with you, Dr. Alexander,' she asked.

"'Certainly,' I said, 'now?'

"'There's something I have to tell you.'

"We stepped off the elevator and walked into an empty room. 'You don't know me,' she stated, 'but I know who you are, and that you took care of Dr. Rice. Tom and I were friends. I worked very closely with him, and I was very distressed when he died so suddenly. I didn't have a chance to say goodbye. I know you might think this is crazy, but I went to see a spiritual counselor, who has a special gift of channeling. She let me know that Tom was fine, and I had a chance to say goodbye. As the channeler relayed the information, she asked, "Who is John?" I told her I wasn't sure but thought it might be you, his doctor. The channeler relayed the message: "Tell John I'm fine, that he understood me well and did the right thing." Does this mean anything to you?' She had no way of knowing about my self doubts—of having interpreted a metaphor from my semi-conscious patient. I'm so thankful I followed my heart."

# THE AWAKENING

One terribly busy day at the hospital, I didn't get a chance to go to lunch until 2:30 PM. The cafeteria only had cold sandwiches left. Walking through the line, I could see that the lunchroom was almost empty. A nurse I vaguely recognized had just sat down at one of the empty tables to eat her lunch. As I set my tray down at her table, she acknowledged me with a half-smile and kept eating.

"Hi. Mind if I join you?" I asked.

"Not at all," she replied.

"Been busy? I hear the hospital is full."

She shook her head and stated, "It's full, I'm way too busy, we are all understaffed, and I'm really having a lousy day." As I nodded sympathetically to her, she continued on, "It all started off this morning when the very first patient I awoke to take vital signs yelled at me."

"For what?" I asked.

"Because I woke her up! This 77-year-old lady claimed that her father had visited last night and that I had interrupted the first good night's sleep she has had since being hospitalized for her stroke."

"Really?" I said. "Her father . . . she said her father visited her?"

"Yes, her dear old daddy came to visit—that's what she said. I think she was hallucinating. Since then, I have had five new admits, all really sick, and no time for a break since 6:00 AM!"

Something about that story caught my interest. We both finished eating and, as we got up to leave, I turned to the nurse and inquired, "Your first patient this morning, do you think she'd mind if I stopped by to visit her?"

"No I don't think she'd mind—especially if she is awake. She rarely has any company."

"What room is she in?"

"219. And good luck!"

I hurried through the rest of my surgical slides and laboratory duties. It was early evening when I walked down to Mrs. Barrow's room, 219. At first I just walked past her door to glance in the room. I could see her lying on her side in bed. The late afternoon sun was blocked by drawn window shades, making the room dusky. I couldn't tell if she was sleeping or not. There were a few "get well" cards on her bedside table but no flowers. I knocked gently and stepped part way into the room. Not wanting to elicit the same reaction the nurse had earlier that day, I quietly called her name, "Mrs. Barrow?"

She was lying there quietly. Her body was still but her eyes were alert. "Yes?" she responded.

"May I talk with you for a few minutes?"

Mrs. Barrow just looked at me as I introduced myself. I walked around the corner of her bed so I could more clearly see her eyes. She waited. So I continued, "I heard you had a wonderful thing happen to you last night."

Her eyes widened. She paused and looked intently at me. "You believe me . . . don't you!"

"Yes," I replied. "I do believe you and would be honored if you would tell me about it."

Taking a deep breath, she smiled and said, "I have been here for over a week now since I had a mild stroke, and I haven't slept well at all on any given night. But last night, as I drifted off to sleep, I was awakened by the most beautiful light. It flooded my room. It was exquisite!" She paused briefly and I noticed the tears streaming down her cheeks. "I was filled with so much joy that words cannot describe it. The light was love—my room was flooded with love and light." She shook her head, "Light or love—it's all the same. I can't explain it, but I was overwhelmed with joy."

"Go on," I gently encouraged.

"I know that my eyes were open; I know I wasn't dreaming, Doctor, because I remember looking at the digital clock at my bedside. It said 12:16."

"I believe you," I said, remembering that first story I had heard so many years earlier.

"Then," she continued, "I saw my father standing next to my bedside and my brother, who died in a farming accident some 30 years ago. They were both smiling so grandly at me that I felt all their love. It just washed over me. Dad sat down on the edge of my bed and I said to him, 'Dad, can I come with you now?'

"He told me, 'Not yet, Dorothy, not just yet. . . .' And I understood why then, but I can't remember now. Then Dad said, 'When it's time, I'll be here to take you home. I love you.'"

"Doctor," Mrs. Barrow said, "I was surrounded by such tremendous love and reassurance. I will never be the same again. I have never felt such peacefulness and calmness. After that, I fell soundly asleep for the first time since being in the hospital—until that darn nurse woke me up so early this morning!"

With that, her daughter walked into the room, so I thanked her and excused myself. She invited me to stop back some time, which I did on several occasions before she was discharged from the hospital.

We visited again one Saturday afternoon about 6 weeks later. She had invited me over for a cup of coffee and we chatted for awhile. She calmly told me that her brother had experienced a severe heart attack shortly after she returned home and that she was caring for him now and cooking his meals. She told me she was certain that this was the reason she had not "gone home" with her father.

When I asked how her experience in the hospital had changed her life, she responded, "Doctor, I will never be the same again. I know that I am dearly loved by God. I often feel the loving presence of my father and brother. I can handle whatever the future brings because I have been 'bathed in the light.'"

# MARGUERITE
# AND HAROLD

My mother, Verda, the youngest of four children, grew up with two sisters and a brother in Sisseton, South Dakota. Their childhood was of a time where the grasshopper plagues, dust bowls, and crop failures were recent memories. Clyde, her father, worked as a common laborer and helped out at a livestock sale barn. Her mother, Maggie, besides raising four children, worked part time as a self-taught bookkeeper and was known to bake the most heavenly cinnamon rolls and cookies in the world. Mother's oldest sister, Marguerite, frequently took care of my mother and they grew very close—a bond that spanned their lifetime.

Marguerite married Harold MacAdaragh, a wonderfully warm, generous, Irish farm boy from Browns Valley, Minnesota. Harold had an open smile and kind heart. Harold and Marguerite eventually moved to Detroit,

Michigan, and raised two daughters. My mother and dad spent so many wonderful days with them. The foursome loved to play cards—from their youthful days in Detroit to Florida in their grand old age.

At age 82, Harold began to experience pain and stiffness in his left upper arm and shoulder. For months he put it off as muscle strain but eventually had to seek medical attention. X rays showed a large tumor of the soft tissues of the arm and, unfortunately, multiple small tumors that had spread to both lungs.

Harold suffered through chemotherapy and radiation therapy for a number of months. The tumors initially subsided but later recurred. Harold decided to stop the therapy and enjoy his remaining days. These golden months were filled with many visits, tears, laughter, and card games. My mother and father traveled to Detroit frequently during that time. On one visit, Harold confided in my father that he was having trouble getting to sleep. It had been Harold's custom for many years to have a small glass of brandy before bedtime, but his doctors had cautioned him not to drink anymore. My physician father gave Harold permission to drink his glass of brandy—in fact, that evening Harold drank several—and all slept better that night.

Throughout this difficult time, Marguerite was his

splendid companion. She always had a twinkle in her eye and a kind word on her lips.

When Harold died later that year, my parents traveled back to Detroit for his funeral—a marvelous tribute for a life well lived.

Marguerite, not unexpectedly, was bereft after the funeral and it seemed she couldn't stop crying. My mother was miserable about leaving her. On the morning of my parents' departure, Marguerite tearfully kissed my mother goodbye. Mother promised to call her when they arrived home later that evening. My mother worried about her sister during the entire trip home.

When Mother dialed the phone number late that night, much to her surprise, Marguerite answered in a clear, calm—even reassuring—voice. My mother asked what had changed. Marguerite proceeded to tell her that after they had left, she was almost beside herself with grief and loneliness. She could not get back to sleep, had wandered around her house, and then decided to tackle a task she had put off for months—cleaning out the cupboard under the kitchen sink! With that accomplished and finally being tired, she laid down mid-morning to rest and promptly fell asleep. No sooner had she fallen asleep, she recounted to my mother, than her beloved Harold appeared to her, kneeling beside her bed. He was filled with a glow of peacefulness. Taking her hand in his, he said, "Marguerite, please don't cry so. I am fine. I am right here with you and I will always love you! And I will be here with you always." Marguerite slept peacefully and contentedly until well after noon. When she awakened, she was overwhelmed with a sense of comfort and calmness that stayed with her for many days. Mother was amazed at the transformation.

Over the next 8 years until her death, Marguerite experienced many dreams of Harold—all of which comforted her and us.

# THE ROBE

I lectured one evening for a group of ophthalmologists and their spouses. The lecture had gone well. I had noticed a tall, slightly graying man smiling brightly and nodding as I spoke. He came up to me afterwards and told his story.

"Doctor, my wife and I were married for over 30 years when she was diagnosed with a rare form of neuroendocrine cancer. We were overwhelmed by how quickly it spread through her body despite all that medicine had to offer. Within a year she was registered in a hospice program and I had a home health aide staying with her during the day so that I could continue my work as a pharmacist. One day when I came home, the aide told me that Martha, my wife, had asked for her 'robe,' but then had quickly added, 'My robe is not ready yet.' I was somewhat puzzled. Little did I realize that Martha's death was imminent—less than 5 days away.

"On the day prior to her death, one of Martha's many friends stopped in to see her. She had become weaker and was telling all of us her vivid dreams and visions. She said, with her eyes shining and wide, that she had seen her robe, that it was white and gleamed and shimmered, and that she was at peace. She shared glimpses of her visions of angels and heaven, shimmering colors, and joy. She was filled with ecstasy by what she saw. I know that she had no regrets about leaving—dying—she just slipped into glory."

"Mr. Nelson," I asked, "how has this affected your life?" Although the tears welled up in his eyes, he appeared resolute.

"I was so uplifted by what she experienced that at the funeral I was, strangely, joyful and sad. I was sad for me, but somehow thrilled at what I had been allowed to glimpse. I feel her with me often. I feel the comfort of her love. Doctor, I don't feel that heaven is way up there somewhere." He pointed up at the ceiling. "I feel that it is right here, now, all around us—that Martha, that heaven, God, is right here. And knowing that has helped me live fully in the months since Martha died. Her life was a gift to so many. Her treasures were her friends, her love, and her wit. She would always end up comforting others and cause them to laugh and enjoy the time with her. I am truly a lucky man!"

# THE VISIT

It was mid-May, 1987, when an extraordinary thing happened to me. Perhaps it was an awakening or maybe an ancient remembering, but my life in many subtle ways has never been the same since. Neale Donald Walsch states in his book, *Conversations With God,* that the best way to cause yourself to remember is to cause another to remember. If that is true, then this entire book has been an effort to remind myself of what I so vividly experienced and knew on that warm, sunny spring afternoon at my farm near Welch, Minnesota.

At that time, I was working with another forensic pathologist at a small but busy hospital perched on the Mississippi River's edge in Hastings, Minnesota. The laboratory was bright and efficient and the staff was cohesive and hardworking. We all had fun practicing laboratory medicine and surgical and forensic pathology. It was my first job since residency.

One day, I noticed a folded up newspaper on the pathology secretary's desk. It caught my eye because the headline read "AIDS is challenge of a lifetime for expert in dying, Elizabeth Kübler-Ross." Dr. Ross' work was well known as pioneering when she described the stages of grieving, from denial and anger through acceptance. As the reporter described Dr. Ross and her background, my attention was riveted when an experience was cited as "proof of the afterlife."

Dr. Ross told the story of an over-the-road trucker who had stopped to help a woman collapsed on the roadway, apparently the victim of a hit-and-run-driver. Her injuries were severe, and as he attempted to comfort the dying woman, she made a request. She asked that the trucker contact her mother, tell her of the circumstances, and tell her that everything was all right because "Dad is already there." The woman died of her injuries.

The trucker was true to his word. He drove 700 miles out of his way to deliver her message because it was impossible to reach the mother by phone. The woman's mother was stunned. It was only then that the trucker learned that the young woman's father had died suddenly and unexpectedly of a heart attack exactly 1 hour before his daughter.

I cannot put into words exactly how I felt after reading the article, but I cut it out and have saved it all these years in the bottom of my jewelry box. I reread the now yellowed page as I wrote this.

That afternoon, I was off work and decided to drive down to my farm, which has always been a refuge for me. It is nestled in the quiet green hills of the Cannon River Valley in the Richard J. Dorrer Memorial Forest. A long winding driveway leads from a seldom traveled dirt road to an old red barn and a very old farmhouse. The walls of the house have heard many good conversations, over many hearty meals, across the years.

I had the afternoon to myself—a rare occurrence. Neither my husband nor dogs had accompanied me. I loved them dearly but treasured the time to myself and was planning a walk and a few hours to quietly read a good book. After making a sandwich, I decided to sit out under the enormous old oak tree that graces the yard and frames the view of the red oak barn. With the heat of the midday sun and the

sound of beetles buzzing in the freshly planted fields, I felt
my eyelids starting to close. A NAP! I thought, this is a perfect afternoon for a nap . . . something that I did not often
allow myself.

I put down the book and climbed upstairs to the bedroom. I remember quickly falling asleep with the ceiling fan
turning lazily above me.

The next thing I remember was startling, even amazing,
but not at all alarming or frightening. Suddenly I found
myself up above my sleeping body. In the next instant, I
knew a place of stunning magnificence. I was aware that I
was composed of light and that I was in a very, very familiar
place surrounded by beings of Light. They all knew me and I
somehow knew them—it was all so incredibly happy—they
welcomed me and embraced me with warmth and infinite
kindness. Then I became aware that we were all intimately
connected with one another. It was as if we were all part of a
bright sparkly sunlit ocean. We sent love and this incredible
brilliant light to one another by just splashing it to each
other. I remember being filled to bursting with happiness,
laughter, and extreme joy—everything was perfect. I understood the meaning of my life. I felt blissfully at home, content, and profoundly peaceful. Perhaps, I am just
remembering it now.

I awoke and found myself back in bed at the farmhouse. The vividness of the experience lingered as I slowly opened my eyes. The ceiling fan was still circling slowly, but the sunlight was low in the sky, casting shadows across the room.

Three hours had passed—it was now late afternoon. I remember to this day that my body felt heavy and slow and that I had trouble moving. It seemed to take a long time to sit up and bring my legs over the edge of the bed. I just sat for 5 or 10 minutes. My heart was awash in the beauty of the experience.

Slowly, I made my way down the stairs to the kitchen. My body felt clumsy and heavy. It was all I could do to make myself a cup of tea. I sat down under the shade of the oak tree. I remember that the evening air was heavy. Tall cumulus summer clouds filled the western sky, creating beautiful sunbeam vistas.

At first, I could not speak of the experience, I was so "filled-up" and overwhelmingly peaceful. Perhaps it was the certainty of a knowing, or remembering. But as I sat under the oak tree, sipping my tea, I felt profoundly different.

I knew then, with absolute certainty, that I was more than just my body. And that we are all deeply and profoundly connected—connected by Love.

# THE LAST DANCE

As often happens, some treasured experiences are shared with me after one of my lectures. This day was no exception. I had just finished lecturing to a group of nurses at a critical care symposium. The previous speaker was a dynamic woman who discussed many new perspectives and hiring practices of current heath care organizations. She had given a wonderful PowerPoint presentation with her computer and many audience members crowded up to talk with her after she finished. The presentation had run at least 10 minutes over the allotted time.

My talk was the last one of the day. I felt at ease with the group and the stories were well received. I walked to the back of the hall and was surprised to see that the previous speaker had stayed to listen. She thanked me and said that she had just one similar experience. It happened early in her career when she was working in the coronary care unit.

As she was reporting for her shift, she saw the cardiac monitor in a patient's room suddenly go from normal sinus rhythm to ventricular fibrillation. She ran into the room—the patient was an elderly widow in her late 70's, and delivered a "precordial thump," a forceful blow to the sternum designed to shock or "startle" the heart back into normal sinus rhythm. Resuscitative efforts were started and the woman was quickly stabilized. The nurse felt proud and pleased to have been of such service.

Later on in the evening as her shift was drawing to a close, she decided to go back and check on the lady. As she walked into the room and introduced herself, she was somewhat surprised when the lady said, "Oh, so you're the one!" "Yes," she said, "I saw the monitor and realized you had slipped into ventricular fibrillation. I ran into your room to help you," she said, not at all expecting what was said next.

"Well, I must admit that I don't quite know if I should be thanking you or not," said the lady. "You see, I was having the most extraordinary dream. My dear husband, who died several years ago, was standing just above the bed," she said, quickly wiping a tear from the corner of her eye. "He put his hand out to me and I took it, and then he lifted me up right out of this bed. Gently, he wrapped his arms around me and we began to dance. He always said he would save the last dance for me. We danced blissfully in each others arms—that is, until you hit me in the chest!"

The nurse looked at me with a smile on her face. "I didn't know what to make of it then, but it's the reason I stayed and listened to your lecture."

As I drove home in rush hour traffic, I, too, hoped that he really did save the last dance for her.

# A HERO'S WELCOME

Several years ago, on the evening before my very first lecture on this subject, I was a nervous wreck. The lecture was for the Minneapolis and St. Paul Surgical Society, an intellectually conservative group called upon daily to make life and death decisions with emotions put aside. I was fearful of how my lecture would be received. It would have been so much easier to speak about forensic pathology.

That night I had a very vivid dream. I was looking in on an enormous gathering filled with literally thousands of people who were feverishly clapping and cheering for someone I could not see. I became aware of a very familiar guiding Presence, standing right beside me. I said to Him, "What is this? A birthday party?" He paused and said, "No." Mystified, I persisted, "Is this a graduation party??" He again answered, "No."

I gazed again. The joy in the place was overwhelming. Amazingly beautiful music filled the place and light beamed from every heart. Love radiated from everyone and beautiful colors filled the air.

"What is it then?" I asked again. In a deep and gentle voice he answered, "Janis, I wanted to show you. . . . This is a celebration for a Life Well Lived." And I marveled . . . and I understood.

I awoke calm, reassured, and ready for the lecture.

In the days and nights that have passed since September 11, 2001, I have wondered what might have awaited our heroes and loved ones who gave their lives.

# PART VI

# THE TAPESTRY OF LIFE

Earth has no sorrow
that heaven cannot heal.

*Thomas Moore*

# AFTER THE STORM

I can see clearly now, the rain is gone
I can see all obstacles in my way
Gone are the dark clouds that had me blind
Gonna be a bright, bright sun-shiny day. . . .

*Johnny Nash*

The night after my beloved grandmother died, 28 years ago, I was awakened in the stillness of the early morning hours when I became aware of her presence at the foot of my bed. She had been diagnosed with breast cancer 4 years earlier, at the age of 85. She had died in Seattle while visiting her son; my mother had flown out to be with her as her condition worsened. Dad had told us of her death and I was devastated. My grandmother and I were very close. When I was a young child, she had lived with my mother and me in California while my father was serving in the Korean conflict. Back then, she was my playmate and sandbox companion; now she was my closest friend and confidante.

I sat up in bed, not at all startled but completely overjoyed! Her presence was familiar, graceful, and reassuring. The evening before I had sobbed and wept thinking I would never see her again. At that moment, she just glowed and looked stunningly beautiful, calm, and younger than before. With a look of supreme Irish knowing, and without even moving her lips, I heard her words, "Janis, tell your mother that I am just fine. And always remember how much I love you." Her presence stayed with me until I fell back to sleep. I awakened with a deep sense of peacefulness and a new awareness. In some ways I have never been the same again. I knew in my heart that my Grandmother lived and that our love was forever.

This beautiful intimate experience in the midst of such shattering grief comforted my heart in a way I couldn't even explain. It seemed to belong to another dimension, deep within. It spoke to my soul, and I somehow recognized that which had been forgotten and felt comforted. This knowing has caused a subtle shift in perspective and a growing awareness of what heals and comforts.

When faced with the death or serious illness of a loved one—whether a parent, son or daughter, spouse, or a long-time friend—we are almost always shaken, often to the core. When the death is unexpected, or sudden, the grief, anger, and confusion can be overwhelming. It can feel as if value or belief systems have failed, leaving one unprepared to go on. I remember a woman who came to my office to obtain a copy of the autopsy report on her father—he had died in a car crash. After answering her questions, she told me that her husband had died several years earlier of heart disease, leaving her alone to care for their 7-year-old son. She told me how bitter she felt and angry with life. "I feel so alone, so abandoned," she said tearfully. "I never knew it would be so hard. Nothing ever prepared me for this."

Everyone has heard these words or felt the pain at some point in their lives. And all know that with time, our grief is tempered. But what actually heals? What helps us find the wisdom to live? The great masters of our time have taught us that our grief honors our love. We are designed to grieve, but not for long. Ultimately, we must trust Life and Love and Hope.

Maybe our grieving hearts echo our bodies' wisdom. Our grief is like an intensely painful wound: it gets our full and immediate attention. The physical wound must be tended, cleaned, and the bleeding stopped. Only then can it be bandaged and the pain relieved. Whether a wounded hand or a wounded heart, the healing comes from within. In the process, time passes, priorities shift, and life proceeds. However, life is different for we have changed.

But how have we changed? A man came to see me after his wife died in the hospital ICU following a long and difficult struggle with cancer. He looked bedraggled and depressed. After explaining the autopsy findings and hospital course, he sat there, folded his hands over his eyes, and wept. "She was the love of my life; I lived for her!" he said. "We met after my first wife died. I sold my house, bought a motor home, and we traveled the country from the Canadian Rockies to the Yucatan Peninsula. It was a dream of a lifetime to have that time with her. I had never ever been so happy! And now she is gone, I have no reason to go on. . . ." he sobbed. For a reason unknown to me I suddenly said, "Do you know how lucky you are?" He looked at me suspiciously. "I talk with so many people about the death of their loved ones, but I can't hardly remember when anyone described such a love to me with such passion and intensity. I think some people wait a whole lifetime to find what you did. You were loved, and you loved grandly.

Somehow I have to believe that your life is richer because of that." He looked at me and I could see that something had changed.

We walked out of the office together and paused at the stairwell before I headed down the hall to the morgue.

"Thank you, Doctor, for everything," he paused, "I had forgotten how lucky I am to have loved like that. And just how much I am loved. . . . I can live with that. I'll remember now, thank you," he said with a smile, then turned and walked up the stairway.

# COMMON THREADS

It's been said that a lifetime can be compared to a tapestry, each experience weaving in a new thread. Perhaps in time, grief strengthens and hones us. Much like a resilient hidden thread, it adds strength and fullness to our lives. If we didn't love, we wouldn't grieve.

I carry these messages with me and try to apply them to my life. I have slowly come to recognize a few common threads. Even so, I am keenly aware that, like each person's life, the tapestry is in the hand of the weaver.

### The thread of Stillness

A death or discovery of a serious illness jars us out of our daily routines. We stop all that we are doing. Other than death, there are few things in life that temporarily relieve us of obligations. Grief seems to have that effect; it stops us and, at times, numbs us. But when sorrow has exhausted us and tears have emptied us, stillness overtakes us. When the mind becomes quiet, the heart can feel. Maybe then our loved ones dance into our awareness and our dreams and delight us. Their presence comforts and fills us with reassurances of their love. Such experiences change lives and heal hearts. Maybe stillness is one of the threads that connect us.

## The thread of Love

A death or serious illness reminds us that all beginnings have an ending, that each interaction with one another may be our last. This reminder has a way of cutting through the "nonessential" stuff of life. It may change what we say or what we do. Maybe like the young woman whose husband was killed in the construction accident, we remember to kiss our loved ones good-bye. Each moment becomes a gift, and time becomes sacred. This remembering may cause us to treat one another more honestly, gently, and deliberately. It seems there is nothing that love cannot heal, and in the presence of love, there is Life, always and forever. Love seems to be the thread that connects All; what is seen with our eyes and felt in our hearts. Ultimately, it must be what connects us with Eternity.

### The thread of Hope

These experiences fill me with a sense of hope. Perhaps when we stop dismissing the awareness of a presence or a synchronicity, we begin to glimpse something more. Many times as I have begun a postmortem examination, I observe how quickly the body disintegrates after death. I marvel at the strength of the Life Force that sustained it. I marvel at the Life Force, God, and feel as though there is so much more to know.

Occasionally I catch a glimpse of what heals—the awareness of our loved one in the whisper of the wind, in the soft beauty of a star gleaming night, or gently dancing into our dreams as we sleep. Why do these connections heal? Perhaps because we must stop to absorb them and be still to observe them. Then we can remember that we are not alone, that we are dearly loved, and all is well.

I am filled with heartfelt appreciation for those who, in the midst of their grief, have spoken of their treasured experiences. I feel honored to share them with others. Many times I have wondered if I would move on as well as those who have been in my care. When something happens to you personally, it hurts deeply. Part of your life is changed forever.

When my mother was urgently admitted to the hospital for heart disease, I was very worried for her welfare and that of my 83-year-old father. They had been married for over 55 years; my physician father appeared both knowledgeable and fragile at the same time. One evening at home during that time, I sat down to rest and reflect on the day's events. My thoughts turned to worry and fear as the fatigue of the day washed over me. I sat at my desk to write but no words would come. So I began to pray. Almost immediately, and somewhat unexpectedly, my head filled with the following words, spoken with such infinite tenderness that tears washed down my cheeks.

"Janis, I love you so. Don't worry, your parents will be fine. At the moments of their death, I will wrap them up in my love and yours, and they will be forever ours."

The comfort, amazement, and relief I felt were overwhelming. I knew instinctively that these words were true and would last me a lifetime.

It is my fondest hope that the wisdoms shared in this book will comfort and remind us of what really heals, knowing we are loved, knowing we are never alone, knowing our loved ones are forever ours.

And if I go
While you're still here . . .
Know that I live on
Vibrating to a different measure
Behind a veil you cannot see through.
You will not see me,
so you must have faith.
I wait for the time when we can
soar together again
both aware of each other.
Until then, live life to its fullest!
When you need me, just whisper
my name in your heart
. . .I will be there

*Author unknown*

# JANIS AMATUZIO, M.D.

trained at the University of Minnesota,
the Hennepin County Medical Center,
and the Medical Examiner's Office in Minneapolis,
Minnesota, before founding Midwest Forensic Pathology, P.A.
Board certified in anatomic, forensic, and clinical pathology,
she is a recognized authority in forensic medicine, and has
developed many courses in topics such as death investigation,
and forensic nursing, and forensic medicine in mortuary sci-
ence. Dr. Amatuzio serves as coroner and a regional resource
for multiple counties in Minnesota and Wisconsin. A
dynamic speaker, she is frequently requested to speak on
"Lessons in Living From Your County Coroner."

COPIES OF THIS BOOK may be obtained by contacting:
Midwest Forensic Pathology, P.A.
3960 Coon Rapids Blvd., LL21
Coon Rapids, Minnesota 55433
763-236-9050
or visit our website at: www.foreverours.com